KEEP SMILING THROUGH

Susan Briggs read Politics, Philosophy and
Economics at Oxford University and over the
years has assembled a fascinating collection of
the ephemera of the Second World War. She
is the wife of Asa Briggs, with whom she was
the co-author of *Cap and Bells*. They live in
Sussex with their four children.

BOOK
PRODUCTION
WAR ECONOMY
STANDARD

THIS BOOK IS NOT PRODUCED IN
COMPLETE CONFORMITY WITH THE
AUTHORIZED ECONOMY STANDARDS.

JOAN ST
ALACE of VARIETIES
NON STOP
EEP SMILING)

SPITFIRE
FIGHTER FUND
Do it NOW

SUSAN BRIGGS

KEEP SMILING THROUGH

Fontana/Collins

I have been helped at many points by Andra Nelki whose knowledge of illustrations, experience of picture research and enthusiasm for the subject of the book have been invaluable, and by Anthony Cohen, my adaptable and imaginative designer. Last, and most of all, I have been helped by my husband who has gone through all the material and problems with me.

First published by George Weidenfeld & Nicolson 1975
First published in Fontana 1976
Copyright © Susan Briggs 1975
Designed by Anthony Cohen

Printed in Great Britain by
Cox & Wyman Ltd,
London, Fakenham and Reading

CONTENTS

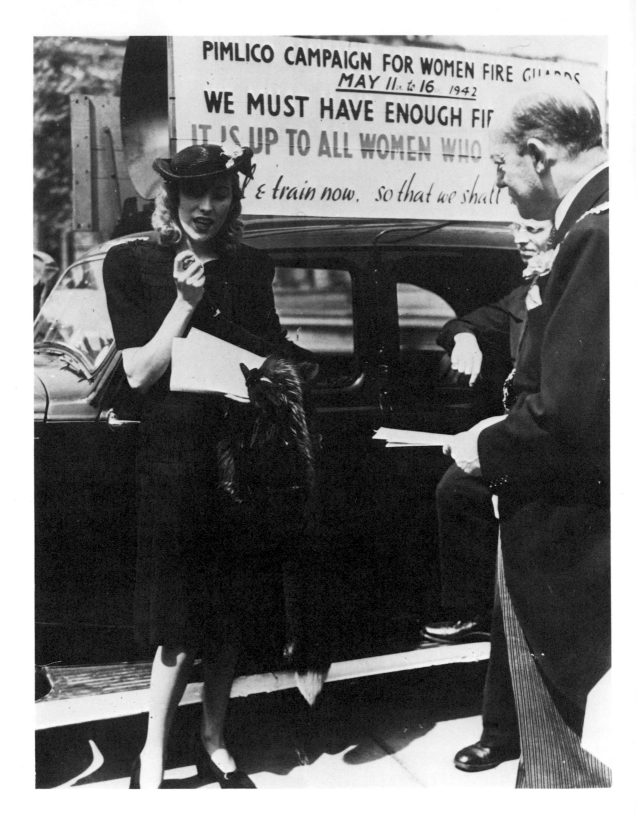

I was very happy to be invited to introduce Susan Briggs's book. The years she recalls and the pictures she has chosen from all kinds of places will evoke many memories. I like too the way in which she has fitted together the pictures of the war and the songs. Many of them were songs I used to sing and which people still want to hear. It would have been good if the book could have included a collection of records, but books can't do this.

The wartime years are an interesting time to look back on, not as dead years, but as years when people were very much alive and when, whatever the sense of danger, they held together. In writing my book about my own story in which the war years played such a great part I have often recalled the experiences which we all shared together, and Susan Briggs certainly catches all the moods, serious and not so serious, of that time. It is fascinating to have all this material about different aspects of wartime ways of life put together in this one book.

To me what mattered most then was the personal touch, so important when people were often separated by huge distances. I would like now to add my own personal touch to Susan Briggs's book.

Yours
Vera Lynn

INTRODUCTION:
IN THE MOOD

September, 1939

S.	✿	**③**	**10**	**17**	**24**
M.	✿	**4**	**11**	**18**	**25**
T.	✿	**5**	**12**	**19**	**26**
W.	✿	**6**	**13**	**20**	**27**
T.	✿	**7**	**14**	**21**	**28**
F.	**1**	**8**	**15**	**22**	**29**
S	**2**	**9**	**16**	**23**	**30**

The pictures in this book come from many different places. They do not pretend to present a comprehensive social history of the Second World War or of what was thought of at the time as 'the Home Front'. Their range is wide enough, however, to demonstrate the particular identity of the war – so different from the First World War – as it was perceived at the time, above all to catch the sense of immediacy.

All the layers of subsequent interpretations (private and public) have been stripped away so that no quotation in this book comes from the period after 1945. It is true, of course, that in the mid-1970s, the selection of pictures and of comments inevitably reflects contemporary interests thirty years on, but there is no pretence in this book that everything is put into perspective. While the war went on, everything was out of perspective, sometimes wildly so. You could not gaze around the corner. There was some intimation, however, that a book might be written in the future – our present – which might even get things wrong.

"I suppose in about thirty years' time people will insist on describing this as the good old days."

It is not only pictures which evoke wartime moods. So, too, do songs, and each chapter in this book – including the title – draws upon songs actually sung during the war. They were not just good (or bad) songs with witty (or banal) words that happened to have been written then. Most of them could not have been written at any other time. To hear them being sung now (and many of them can still be heard, if only on records) is to

establish the right reactions, to be 'in the mood'. I have gone back in the case of the songs in this book, as in the case of the pictures and the verbal quotations of reactions at the time, to the invaluable comments of *Melody Maker*, one of my favourite sources; to remarks made inside the BBC, which had a powerful influence on what songs were actually sung (though not necessarily on the words sung to them); and, above all, to the words of the songs themselves from 'Der Führer's Face' to 'You'd be so Nice to Come Home to'. 'There'll Always be an England' (written before war broke out in the spring of 1939) was already being treated as a kind of new national anthem as early as January 1940 by the Performing Right Society on the same rates and the same terms as 'Land of Hope and Glory'.

Poetry is a more difficult medium to interpret, not least since even at the time, when large (even record) numbers of books of poems were being published and read, there was a feeling (articulated, for example, in *The Listener*) that the Second World War, unlike the First, was not inspiring the poet. Its epic scale seemed to mute the lyric voices of poets who had been able to sing in the trenches. Some of the verse which sold most copies, like *The White Cliffs* by Alice Duer Miller (which first appeared in February 1941: compare the popular song 'The White Cliffs of Dover', also of American origin) interpreted the Second War through the First and brought Americans over to Britain (in fancy) before Franklin D. Roosevelt sent them over in reality after Pearl Harbor:

Say is this chicken feed honey?
Say does it rain every day?
Say, lady, isn't it funny
Everyone drives the wrong way?

It was not a poet but one of the main pillars of *The Economist* and the *News Chronicle*, Sir Walter Layton, who wrote the introduction to the English paperback of *The White Cliffs* and his words, too, still convey their rhetorical immediacy. 'Mrs Miller, in her brilliant and moving poem, does not attempt to gloss over our social inequalities, our insularity, our conceit, our "stodginess". [Compare J. B. Priestley.] Yet no English reader of this book can fail to be touched by the fineness of her perception as her story moves to its climax, and she answers the question whether it is worth while to make the great sacrifice in order that England may live.'

I have set out in my book to deal with the successive phases of the later war – when it was not just a question of whether England might live but of whether Russia might live too ... and when America was making the vital contribution, economic and military, to the actual winning of the war. Yet although I have taken account of time – the war was a very long one with clearly defined phases – I have not followed a strictly chronological treatment throughout. One chapter, 'Over There', sets out material about Britain's wartime visitors, most of them – not all of them – treated as guests. Yet in every chapter, not least that on the war effort, 'Dig, Dig, Dig to Victory', material is necessarily included about 'foreign contributions'. As for the English (not to speak of the Scots, Welshmen or Ulstermen), they liked to think they were nicer, more sensible and positive, less complaining and above all more united during the war than at any other time. Indeed, looking back in perspective J. B. Priestley has written recently, 'The British were absolutely at their best in the Second World War. They were never as good, certainly in my lifetime, before it, and I'm sorry to say they've never been so good after it.'

One chapter of my book deals with the hopes for the future – grounded in wartime 'solidarity'. It could have been called 'My Dreams are Getting Better all the Time', instead of 'It's a Lovely Day Tomorrow', though the lyric of the former song deals explicitly only with private futures. It is fascinating in relation to wartime songs to trace the social (even political) undertones of love songs which pretend to be completely private – not just (obviously) 'My Lovely Russian Rose' or 'I Left my Heart at the Stage Door Canteen' but 'Mem'ries Live Longer than Dreams', which might have been the title of this whole book.

Many of the non-musical sounds of war linger in the memory although they cannot be reproduced in this book. One of them at least, however, the sound of the siren, has become a symbol of the whole war. It was a new sound in 1939, but it has been heard more often since 1945 (on records and radio and television programmes) than it was even at the time. One of the best diaries of the war years – and authentic diaries (not autobiographies, retrospective souvenirs recollected in tranquillity)

THE CHANGING FACE OF BRITAIN
XIV.—ENGLISHMAN'S HOUSE

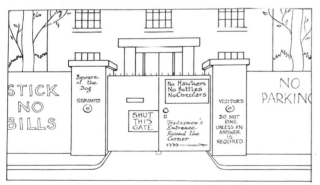

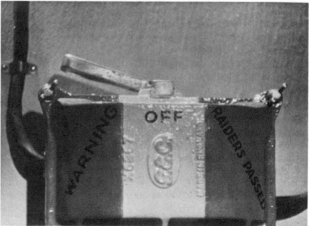

are one of the main primary sources for this book – is called *The Siren Years* (1974). Its author, Charles Ritchie, later to become one of Canada's most distinguished diplomats, was then a young second secretary in the Canadian High Commission in London.

Diaries of men and women who never became distinguished – though a few of them may have hoped during the war years that they might become so – are necessary reading. A manuscript preserved in the London Museum is superbly direct. 'A few weeks back I recorded my opinion that there would be no war,' wrote the eighty-five-year-old diarist on 2 September 1939, 'and added

August 1939

As I look out of my window overlooking Queens Club, I see, what looks like a gigantic elephant but is really a barrage balloon.

We are everywhere prepared for war and quite rightly. At the same time I will put on record that, in my opinion there will be no war as far as England is concerned.

I shall look very 'foolish when the war starts.'

that I should look very foolish when the war starts. Today England declares war on Germany or rather on Hitler and I am looking very foolish. Unfortunately this causes no noticeable change in my facial expression and no one has commented on it. There are, in fact, very few people left in London to comment on anything. The suburbs of London are quiet as disused cemeteries . . .'

There is an irresistible urge to read on. Such diaries are precious, too, because many of them were victims of the wartime salvage campaign – war casualties in a great cause. You were told frequently that you might well have a sack-load of paper in your house and if you possessed 'a magpie hoard' of old programmes, photographs, clippings, post-cards and so on – all the things I most treasure – 'to be ruthless and to keep only the prize pieces'. Such 'prize pieces' tend to be completely unrepresentative, and it is consoling to know that some people's private magpie instincts triumphed over public guidance.

There is some material in this book which could not have been shown during the war because it would never have escaped the censor's blue pencil. There is some, too, which only looks significant because we know what happened after the war was over. There is other material, however, which was safely rooted in its own soil. 'However brave we try to be we invariably quake with fear. War has come upon us . . . These are the grim days, yet our God can still step in, in a mysterious, perhaps, but miraculous way, to draw the nations to Himself.' (From the diary of a Midlands housewife, September 1939.)

Words, if not prayers, are the stock-in-trade of historians, even more than deeds and there is a tendency for them (assisted by reviewers) to treat pictures as decoration and to ignore songs altogether. This book uses both as evidence, along with more 'reputable' kinds of evidence. It also deals quite deliberately with 'trivia'. Mollie Panter-Downes, a superb witness, whose *London War Notes* were written for the *New Yorker*, described 'a country-dwelling lady' who in May 1944 was warned by the contractor who was carrying out urgent plumbing work in her house that he and his mate were all Home Guards and that if the Germans came they would have to drop her new water tank in the middle of her lawn so that she would be left bathless until the war was over. 'It is often in just such a ridiculous way,' she notes, 'that English families begin to realize what it may be like to have the Battle of Europe right on their doorsteps, involving not only big and historic

On the bill-boards

At the easel: the War Artists

Women Railway Porters in Wartime by William Roberts.

Ruby Loftus screwing a breech-ring by Laura Knight.

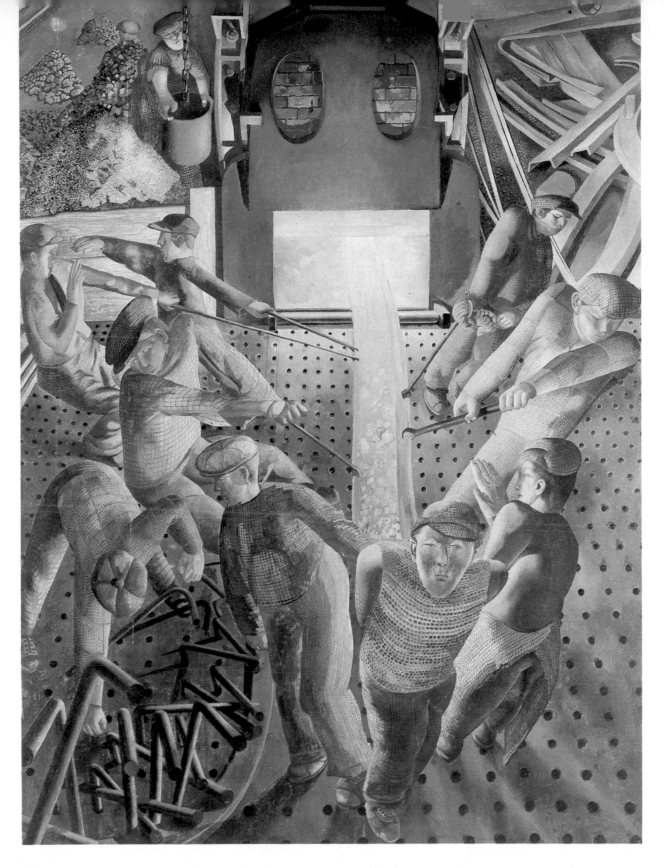

Shipbuilding on the Clyde, Burners by Stanley Spencer.

In the packets

CHURCHMAN'S CIGARETTES

THE STIRRUP HAND PUMP

CHURCHMAN'S CIGARETTES

LIGHT TRAILER FIRE-PUMP IN ACTION

CHURCHMAN'S CIGARETTES

ANTI-AIRCRAFT GUN

CHURCHMAN'S CIGARETTES

WINDOW PROTECTION AGAINST BLAST

CHURCHMAN'S CIGARETTES

SUPPLY DEPOT FOR RESPIRATORS

CHURCHMAN'S CIGARETTES

WINDOW PROTECTION

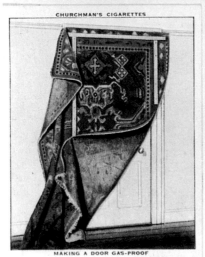

CHURCHMAN'S CIGARETTES

MAKING A DOOR GAS-PROOF

CHURCHMAN'S CIGARETTES

REPRESENTATION OF BALLOON
BARRAGE FOR DEFENCE OF LONDON

CHURCHMAN'S CIGARETTES

TESTING FOR GAS CONTAMINATION

issues but also small and homely ones like baths, trains, the morning paper and the day's milk.'

Sometimes the story of an object can be almost as moving as the story of a person . . . and sometimes, during the Blitz in particular, people might seem like objects. 'A few dark huddled bodies were round about, and right in front of me were two soldiers . . . One was propped up against the wall with his arms dangling by him like a rag doll.' Pictures in words sometimes survive where there are no real pictures. Yet there has never been a war in history where (even though there was no television) more pictorial evidence has survived . . . sometimes topical newspaper pictures which were never taken with any historical intent; sometimes snapshots, which if they had any historical interest were thought of as private history in the making (although private photography was discouraged – in some circumstances banned – during the war. Films were difficult to buy and even if you found one you risked arrest as a Fifth Columnist if, for example, you were spotted taking a photograph of a wrecked aircraft); sometimes posters which carried urgent public messages (*Modern Publicity in War* was even the title of an excellent book published in 1941 with very pertinent observations by John Gloag); sometimes pictures by war artists deliberately painted for the historical record. The War Artists' Scheme followed a successful precedent of the First World War – as the surviving pictures in the Imperial War Museum (to which I am deeply indebted) show. Yet there was a difference in approach as well as in style – and content – as the war artists of the Second World War found themselves able, in Sir Kenneth Clark's words, 'to go on painting with a clear conscience'.

The parallel between the First and the Second World Wars was particularly strong in 1939 when the relatively recent experience of the first great twentieth-century war was fresh in people's minds. There was a backward look as 'then' and 'now' suggested innumerable comparisons and contrasts. The biggest contrast was the unprecedented fear in 1939 of immediate and devastating air attack. There seemed to have been a time in the First World War when 'air raids were fun', to quote the title of an article in the *ARP and AFS Review* (a knowledgeable source): now another writer in the same magazine said in 1939 (quoting his experience of the Spanish Civil War) that there were immediate 'dangers and horrors in store'. There was also a difference in the media of communication: there had been no *ARP and AFS Review* in 1914 but then there had been no BBC – and only a very limited cinema industry.

Any examination of 'then' and 'now' quickly turned into a further examination of 'alike' and 'different' and the second element in the bi-focalism of 1939 was the product of years of pre-war preparation for the war before 1939, however in-

"It's a battle-course for official war artists."

Black leaves are piled against the roaring weir;
Dark closes round the manor and the hut;
The dead knight moulders on his rotting bier,
And one by one the warped old casements shut.

For what happened after September 1939 – the surprises as well as the inevitabilities – this book provides a selective record. Even at the time, as in retrospect, the two wars tended to get merged into one – part of the great twentieth-century divide.

The account I have presented should be supplemented by Angus Calder's *The People's War, 1939–1945* (1969), an indispensable book – and he actually *remembered* less of it than I do; the huge anthology edited by Desmond Flower and James Reeves, *The War* (1960); Norman Longmate's *How We Lived Then* (1971), a fascinating compilation, based, unlike mine, largely on people's memories; Arthur Marwick's *Britain in the Century of Total War* (1968). Professor Marwick is the professional historian of war *par excellence*; and my husband's *The War of Words* (1970) which is far more than a history of the BBC.

It has been a chastening thought in preparing this book that we are now further separated in time from the Second World War than our ancestors were from even the beginning of the First World War when war broke out in 1939.

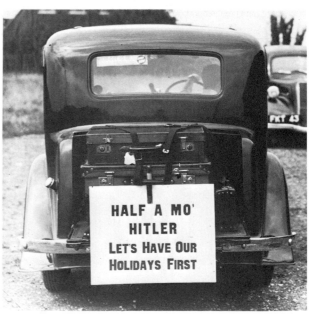

adequate it might have been. Some time between 1918 and 1938 the shadow of the First World War crossed the shadow of the Second. As E. M. Forster put it, drawing the contrast perhaps too sharply, 'The twenties react after a war and recede from it; the thirties are apprehensive of a war and are carried towards it.' Certainly during the 1930s fear and care, exploited by propaganda (the latter channelled into the ARP [Air Raid Precautions]), were blended until in the year between Munich and the outbreak of war it began to be felt increasingly strongly that there was no other outcome than war. There was a 'phoney peace' before there was a 'phoney war' . . . and almost everyone was ready in September 1939. The immediacies of that month can be well expressed pictorially. They are also caught, however, in the immediate documentation, much of it collected and preserved by Mass Observation, a magnificent and still largely untapped source. 'We could eat no breakfast hardly, and just waited with sweating palms and despair for 11 o'clock.' The poet Alun Lewis chose different language to describe autumn 1939:

WE'LL MEET AGAIN

"Now I want you to promise me you're all going to be really *good* little evacuees and not worry his Lordship."

We'll meet again
Don't know where, don't know when,
But I know we'll meet again
Some sunny day.

'What comforts do the men need most?' a war correspondent asked an infantry major in France 'under a sodden sky' in November 1939. The reply was immediate. 'The girls they left behind them.'

All wars are times for saying goodbye, but the first people to say goodbye in 1939 were not the soldiers of the British Expeditionary Force, or the airmen, but the children. Evacuation came before mobilization. 'Surely if war comes, it would be better for families to stick together and not go breaking up their homes?' was another question many people were asking as the government evacuation scheme took shape in July 1939. Yet the children went in their thousands – usually, like private soldiers, they knew not where – into the so-called 'reception areas' – 827,000 schoolchildren, along with 103,000 teachers and helpers. 'It is an exodus bigger than that of Moses,' Walter Elliott, the Minister of Health, exclaimed. 'It is the movement of ten armies, each of which is as big as the whole Expeditionary Force.'

Some children did not leave their mothers behind them. 524,000 children under school-age and their mothers, as well as 12,000 expectant mothers, went out into the unknown together. Evacuation was thought to be least successful when the mothers, 'pathetically bored and home-sick', were with their children. The reactions of the fathers left behind have not been recorded. But many of the mothers – and the children – very quickly returned to their homes. Some had not been able to stand the ' 'orrible bloomin' quiet' of the countryside. More could not stand the people with whom they were billeted. After all the bombs were *not* falling, and the government, not yet imbued with the Dunkirk spirit and as mean as any pre-war government, imposed six shillings a week parental contributions at the end of October.

The mass evacuation of the first days of the war was not the only time during the war that the children – with or without their mothers – were on the move, though it was the one which seared minds and spirits most and lingered longest in the memory. There was another round of evacuation in the summer of 1940, this time, as invasion threatened, from the coastal regions between Norfolk and Sussex as well as the big cities. By then the remnants of the BEF were back in Britain meeting their wives and sweethearts (if they were lucky) far sooner than anyone would have prophesied. There were some left behind in the prison camps who were penning their own versions of Vera Lynn's 'We'll Meet Again' without the assistance of composers or lyric writers:

Keep smiling, don't be blue dear,
My thoughts are all of you dear;
I would feel so low
If I thought that you were shedding tears, so
Keep smiling, don't you cry, dear
Or you'll have me crying too.
We're like birds of a feather
Very soon we'll be together, so
Keep smiling, keep me smiling too.

These were to be the kind of words troops, outside as well as inside prison, liked to sing during the Second World War, rejecting to the distaste of quite a lot of influential people (including Lady Reading, the energetic founder of the WVS), the rousing marching songs of the First World War. The desert war in 1941 and 1942, sustained – indeed heightened – the mood; and it was the first troops to leave their wives and sweethearts behind to fight the Italians and then Rommel who first romanticized the fact of separation.

You're in my mind
I did not bring you there
You should be where my hands can touch your hair.

'Underneath the lamplight' seemed far more nostalgic than 'keeping the home fires burning' . . . and the more professional the soldiers became – they were very different from their First World War counterparts in the trenches – the more their songs expressed universal hopes and fears. 'Lili Marlene' belonged to every soldier, British or German, separated from his loved ones.

The poetry of separation, expressed in the romantic verse of the songs was very different from the prose of evacuation expressed in the brutal realism of some of the first exchanges between evacuees and their (often unwelcoming) hosts. James Agate quoted in his wartime diary in December 1939 an extract from a letter from a friend in the country. 'There are six evacuated children in our house. My wife and I hate them so much that

we have decided to *take away* something from them for Christmas.' The language of the letter was not a pontifical Agate concoction. The WVS, which did so much to assist evacuation in its first great contribution to the war effort, could have published a whole anthology along the same lines:

I am sorry to have to write to you, but I feel it is my duty to do so on behalf of your children, for my wife has not time to write as her time is taken up first with the children then with their clothes, also the vermin that have been in their heads for that is the worst trouble of all for my wife has got some in her own head which I think is wicked for if you are used to being verminous we are not, for we do not blame the children, the fault rests with their parents if you can call them such.

This was plain speaking from one working-class parent (rural) to another (metropolitan). Just as often there were plain misunderstandings as social classes who had remained carefully separate were pushed into confrontation through the evacuees.

Pockets of real feudalism and favouritism came to light in the process of billeting. The weak links

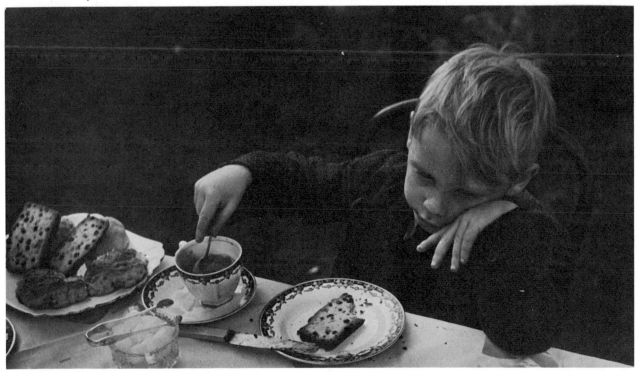

in evacuation were often the billeting officers, usually chosen from local big-wigs. To quote a confidential report by the headmaster of a school evacuated to the west of England:

They [the billeting officers] will not billet children on their friends, so the cottages have evacuees while the large houses do not. In cases where children *are* in the large houses, they are usually left entirely to the maids, who thus get the extra work. One billeting officer actually said to me 'We might as well give the cottagers the chance of making a little money, and they do so like having the children'... In many cases the billeting officers are the owners of these (tied) cottages. The people living in them find it very difficult to refuse to have evacuees. They probably work for him as gamekeepers, gardeners, chauffeurs, labourers etc. The feudal system is still in full swing in these districts and the cottagers dare not refuse to have children.

Evacuation spotlighted all kinds of social and psychological problems – from bed-wetting to serious malnutrition, ignorance of diet, disease –

BEVERAGES AND FOOD

1

Can that be the Rectory?

and some of the shifts in social policy during and after the Dunkirk summer were to be inspired by the new knowledge. Yet the children's views were not always quite the same as the views of their

Embarkation leave

Sheila carries daddy's gas-mask,
Peter carries daddy's gun.
Mother's chattering on and laughing
As if parting were just fun.

She's put apples in his pocket,
He's got photos in his book,
When he isn't busy fighting,
He'll have time to have a look.

parents. Boys evacuated from Southampton only began to cheer up when air battles raged over Dorset. They felt, their headmaster said, as if they were 'in things' now. He quoted one of his pupils: 'It's just as dangerous as Southampton. Now I can get my own souvenirs.' 'Satisfaction was complete,' he concluded, 'when an ME 109 actually crashed in a field . . . especially when the Air Ministry, having taken what it wanted of the remains, said that anyone could clear the rest away. Much of the wreckage was brought to the school for the salvage scheme.'

The future of air battles determined desperately who would or could not meet again – and in what conditions. Going in to action was 'going to the movies'. The 'party' was a very special version of a good time being had by all. 'Embarkation leave' might mean meeting for the first – and last – time, *not* meeting again. The lovely (or unlovely) weekend, the brief encounter, became a common experience for all the services – and for lots of civilians too. Some of the brief encounters led to marriage, however. A Camden Town jeweller sold thirty wedding rings in two days during the first week of war, against the normal three or four. But whether you were married or not, there was always doubt not only about whether you would meet again, but when. 'Looks like another bloody hundred years war' was a remark overheard in a Blackpool pub.

The war correspondent, J. L. Hodson, who interviewed the infantry major in France in November 1939 had served in the First World War, and when he set foot in France again, twenty-four years to the month after his first arrival, he wrote in his diary, 'I had never thought to set out on that adventure twice.' There were others, like Antoine de St Exupéry (who published his *Flight to Arms* in 1942), who looked at the war differently.

There is a great danger in this war. But if we are among those that get back, we shall have nothing to tell . . . war is not a true adventure. It is a mere *ersatz*. Where ties are established, where problems are set, where creation is stimulated – there you have adventures. But there is no adventure in heads-or-tails, in betting that the toss will come out life or death.

GOVERNMENT EVACUATION SCHEME

The Government have ordered evacuat[ion] of school children.

If your children are registered [for] evacuation send them to their assem[bly] point at once.

If your children are not registered a[nd] you wish them to be evacuated, [the] teachers or the school keeper will help y[ou]

If you do not wish your children [to] be evacuated you must not send them [to] school until further notice.

Posters notifying the arrival of parties [in] the country will be displayed at the schools [at] which the children assembled for evacuati[on]

. were the children'

MOTHERS
Send them out
of London

Give them a chance of greater safety and health

It might be YOU!

CARING FOR EVACUEES
IS A NATIONAL SERVICE

ISSUED BY THE MINISTRY OF HEALTH

In early September 1939 thousands of unaccompanied schoolchildren from 'danger' areas set out for the unknown, lonely, if labelled (*see below*). Their only link with home was an officially-issued printed and franked postcard to be sent to parents on arrival with notification of their address. One surviving card ran, 'Dear Mum, I hope you are well. I don't like the man's face much. Perhaps it will look better in daylight. I like the dog's face best.' Government posters (including this one (*left*) with an imaginary back-drop of the as yet non-existent Blitz), backed by leaflets, attempted to persuade parents to let their children be evacuated – and stay evacuated – and told foster-parents that caring for evacuees was patriotic war-work. Some children were left behind, like these Smethwick children watching their friends go (*below left*).

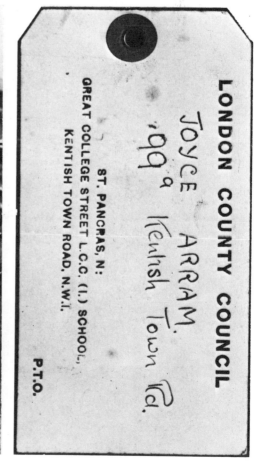

LONDON COUNTY COUNCIL

Joyce ARRAM.
'99 a Kentish Town Rd.

ST. PANCRAS, N:
GREAT COLLEGE STREET L.C.C. (I.) SCHOOL,
KENTISH TOWN ROAD, N.W.I.

P.T.O.

'Home and away'

Britons living abroad (*top left*) crowded into the Westminster Passport Office at the rate of 20,000 a day saying that they would quickly return 'to help'. They whistled 'Tipperary' and 'Blighty' in the queues.

Americans found their shipping office closed and passages sold out on 4 September (*above right*).

Not everyone who got away got very far. The *Athenia* was torpedoed and many lives were lost (*right and opposite below*). This was the first great shock of the war and did nothing to help Hitler's reputation.

Late Morning Edition

News Chronicle

No. 29,122   ONE PENNY   MONDAY, SEPTEMBER 4, 1939

Britain and France at War with Germany

BRITISH LINER TORPEDOED
REPORTED SUNK

Athenia With 1,400 on Board Feared Lost 200 Miles West of Hebrides

THE Donaldson Liner Athenia, with 1,400 passengers on board, was torpedoed yesterday 200 miles west of the Hebrides. She was on her way to Canada.

Reports, so far unconfirmed, state that the Athenia has sunk.

The Athenia is a ship of 13,581 tons and is registered at Glasgow.

The Athenia was recently reconditioned on an extensive scale and had been in the builders' hands for four months.

GENERAL IRONSIDE, aged 59
Chief of Imperial General Staff

GENERAL KIRKE, aged 62
Commander-in-Chief, Home Forces

LATE

TORPEDOE

American states that t number of citizens retu on the Athe the exact nu known.

They were us route home only accommo could find.

Ministry of stated at 5 morning; t official infor ceived by the was that th sinking rapid

WARSAW WILD WITH JOY AT BRITISH DECISION

From **WILLIAM FORREST**
News Chronicle Special Correspondent

WARSAW, Sunday.

POLAND went delirious with joy when she learned today she was not going to fight alone.

In the memory of the oldest citizens of Warsaw, who have seen the Polish nation reborn and victorious in war, there has never been anything to compare with the demonstrations in the streets today.

LORD GORT, C.-IN-C.

The Bremen Captured?

MR CHAMBERLAIN speaking from the Cabinet

NG'S
LL TO
MPIRE

Getting away from it all

In October 1940 Princess Elizabeth broadcast in *Children's Hour* to children evacuated to the Empire and the United States: 'My sister, Margaret Rose, and I feel so much for you, as we know from experience what it means to be away from those we love most of all.'
(The princesses had remained in Scotland when war broke out and the King and Queen returned to London.) 'My sister is by my side, and we are both going to say goodnight – come on Margaret! Goodnight – Goodnight and good luck to you all.'

At the time of the broadcast, the official scheme (responsible for evacuating only 2,700 evacuees abroad) had already come to an abrupt and tragic end when the *City of Benares* was torpedoed with the loss of 73 'seavacuees'.

The playing fields of Malvern

Whole institutions – schools, government departments and the BBC itself– were evacuated to 'safe' areas. St Paul's Boys' School (*above*) moved to the country, Cheltenham doubled up with Shrewsbury and Dulwich with Tonbridge. According to one apocryphal story, two schools had changed places to their mutual satisfaction. Malvern College (*right*) made the grandest change – to Blenheim Palace (reflecting without knowing it the importance of radar research going on in its commandeered premises: the Second World War was said to have been won on the playing-fields of Malvern).

Oxford in 1940 was 'swarming with disoriented hordes, the newly-acquired wartime population (27,000 above normal) composed of evacuees, war-workers, refugees, passing visitors and resident foreigners'. Most colleges had a cuckoo in the nest: thus, Balliol (*opposite right*) housed the Royal Institute for International Affairs, and Ruskin College a maternity hospital. The Polish Courts of Law and the Slade School of Art added a cosmopolitan and bohemian flavour to the academic life.

'All change'

Many animals were evacuated too – if not sent to the gas chamber. In September 1939 a *Times* advertisement offered 'a few approved dogs full board and country walks; gas-proof dug-out and every care for 15s a week'.

In June 1940 livestock were evacuated from 'vulnerable areas' (*left*) but their troubles were not necessarily over when they reached a 'safe area'. Land girls reported young evacuees fitting their gas masks on sheep and then running away.

The oldest and most valuable 'evacuees' were the masterpieces of the National Gallery. They spent a quiet war deep in a North Wales quarry (*below left*). When they re-emerged in 1945 Louis MacNeice wrote:

> The Kings who slept in caves are awake and out,
> The pictures are back in the Gallery;
> Old Masters twirl their cadenzas, whisper and shout.

"Balliol may be a bit earlier, but this is one of the oldest Ministries in the University."

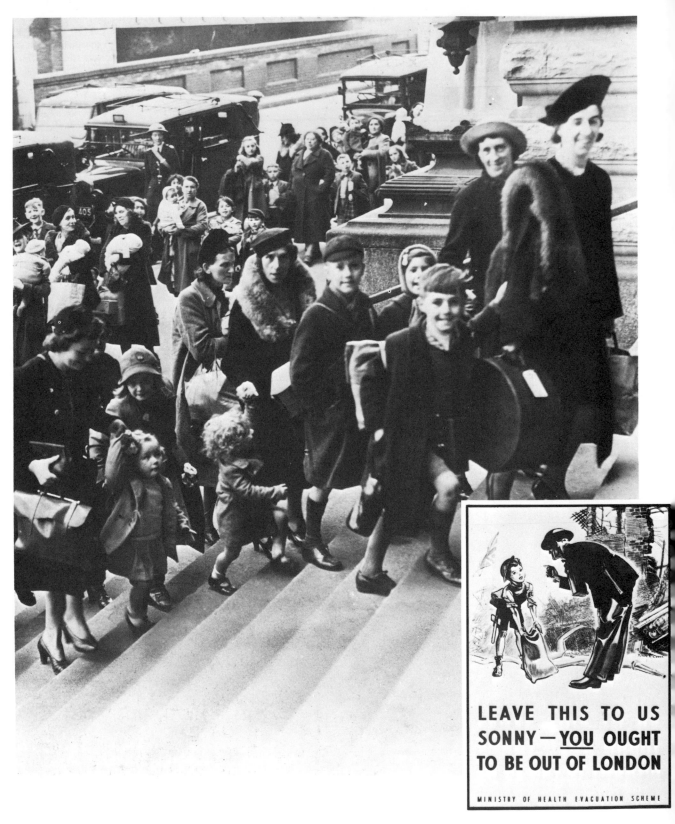

LEAVE THIS TO US
SONNY — YOU OUGHT
TO BE OUT OF LONDON

MINISTRY OF HEALTH EVACUATION SCHEME

. after Dunkirk'

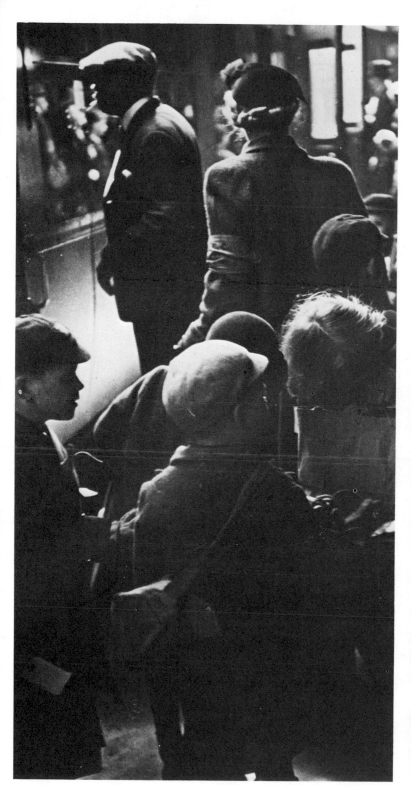

After Dunkirk, offers to take British children poured in from the Dominions and the USA. Somewhat reluctantly – in view of the shortage of shipping – the Government introduced a scheme to send children overseas which was organized by 'Corb' (Children's Overseas Reception Board). By imposing a quota – three-quarters of the children were to come from state schools – it hoped to quash socialist complaints that only 'the children of the rich' had been able to go abroad to safety. When over 200,000 applications for passages had been received by early July, Churchill referred contemptuously to the 'stampede from this country'. This attitude was shared by many older potential evacuees: 'I would rather be bombed to fragments than leave England,' wrote one boy in a letter to the press.

THIRD

'Goodnight children everywhere'

(Gracie Fields 1939 song hit)

These evacuees and their foster-mother (*right*), photographed in November 1939, look happy and settled. Yet in September many of the poorest evacuees, used to sharing their parents' bed (or even sleeping under it), found bed-time a strange experience. In York James Agate's brother reported of some evacuees from Durham: 'They refuse to sleep *in* a bed. They will sleep *under* it . . . Beds, they say, are for dead people – they aren't going to be laid out yet!'

Other children, evacuated to stately homes (*below*), lived in grander but less cosy surroundings . . . like Lady Pembroke's converted bedrooms in 'Bachelors' Row' at Wilton House.

Not only the evacuees grumbled. Michael Barsley described ladies who:

Inspired by Britain's glorious cause
With seven maids to do the chores
Gather round at country teas
  And grouse about evacuees.

'The cow is a mamal'

Many evacuees were seeing the country for the first time: The nine o'clock news on 29 October 1939 ended with an essay by a ten-year-old East London evacuee:

'The cow is a mamal. It has six sides, right, left, an upper and below. At the back it has a tail, on which hangs a brush. With this it sends the flies away so that they do not fall into the milk. The head is for the purpose of growing horns and so that the mouth can be somewhere. The horns are to butt with, and the mouth is to moo with. Under the cow hangs the milk. It is arranged for milking. When people milk, the milk comes and there is never an end to the supply. How the cow does it I have not yet realized but it makes more and more. The cow has a fine sense of smell, one can smell it far away. This is the reason for the fresh air in the country.

The man cow is called an ox. It is not a mamal. The cow does not eat much but what it eats it eats twice so that it gets enough. When it is hungry it moos and when it says nothing it is because all its inside is full up with grass.'

One famous *Punch* cartoon of April 1940 showed an evacuee child greeting her visiting mother: 'This is Spring, Mummy, and they have one every year down here.'

(*Left*) Paintings by pupils of Mary Speaight, evacuated from Limehouse to Somerset.

'Keep them happy, Keep them safe'

(Government evacuation slogan, 1940)

By January 1940 3 out of 4 evacuees had gone home. The lack of air raids, homesickness and (after October 1939) the Government's demand for a small parental contribution towards the support of evacuated children all encouraged the great drift home. In efforts to persuade at least the mothers of unaccompanied children to leave them in 'safe' areas, the Government issued warning posters (*right*) and special 'Visit to Evacuee' cheap day return railway tickets for parents (*far right*).

Such efforts failed to shatter phoney war complacency: when (in February 1940) parents in danger areas were asked to state whether they wished their children to be moved to the country when attacks started, only a quarter even bothered to reply. By May 1940 – just before the second post-Dunkirk round of evacuation – very few evacuees remained in the country. In spring 1940 E. Gabain painted (*below*) some of the few evacuees who 'stayed put'.

DON'T do it, Mother –

LEAVE THE CHILDREN WHERE THEY ARE

ISSUED BY THE MINISTRY OF HEALTH

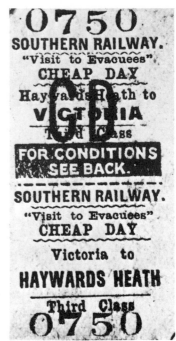

0750
SOUTHERN RAILWAY.
"Visit to Evacuees"
CHEAP DAY
Haywards Heath to
VICTORIA
Third Class
FOR CONDITIONS SEE BACK.
SOUTHERN RAILWAY.
"Visit to Evacuees"
CHEAP DAY
Victoria to
HAYWARDS HEATH
Third Class
0750

Saying goodbye to the billeting officer

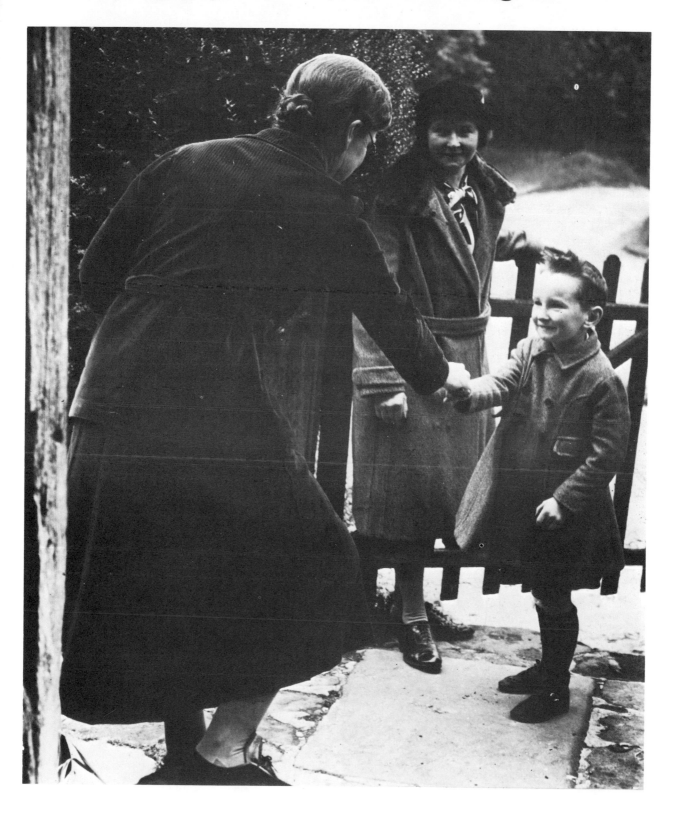

'Kiss the Boys Goodbye'

''e wants to get married, so 'e's applying for passionate leave' (*right*).

'Sending soldiers off to war, 1939 version, is a dark and secret business shorn of all *Cavalcade* trimmings of flags, running children, and military bands playing "The Girl I Left Behind Me",' wrote the *New Yorker*'s London Correspondent. Sometimes 'the Girl' was in uniform herself as in this still from a 'careless talk' propaganda film of 1940 (*below right*). The reality was usually less glamorous (*below left*), the sadness of parting intensified by the anxious prospect of subsisting on the miserable serviceman's dependants' allowance.

Up the social scale *Vogue* gave advice on how to welcome the soldier home: 'Home on leave. Be ready, then, to greet him. Now, if ever, beauty is your duty. Now, if ever, buy with crystal-clear conscience the clothes that will charm him. Remember . . . none but the fair deserves the brave . . . Take him to the newest, nicest restaurants. Encourage your cook to excel herself at home . . .'

WE'RE GONNA HANG OUT THE WASHING ON THE SIEGFRIED LINE

We're gonna hang out the washing on the
   Siegfried line
Have you any dirty washing, mother dear?
We're gonna hang out the washing on the
   Siegfried line
'Cos the washing day is here.

On 3 September 1939 most people in England (with Munich only a year before) knew more about 'dirty washing' than about Siegfried. But they were soon singing two breezy Siegfried Line songs with exactly the same theme (two lyric writers having been simultaneously inspired by the same *Daily Express* cartoon). The one that is forgotten was 'I'm sending you the Siegfried Line to hang your washing on'. There were no intimations in September 1939 of Dunkirk, the event which made the Germans, who had never liked the song before, pick it up and restore it with mocking words, a new Siegfried idyll in a minor key.

Between September and May there was more farce than opera once the Poles had been brutally overwhelmed. The French invented the phrase *drôle de guerre*, the Americans 'phoney war'. Senator Borah was said to have been responsible for the American label. Other Americans and Englishmen talked of a new 'Bore War', particularly now that the theatres and cinemas were closed and the BBC was doing nothing to alleviate the gloom of the early blackout. One listener commented that the tone of news announcers suggested that they were 'understudying for Cassandra on the walls of Troy' . . . 'Rummest war I ever knew', were characteristic words recorded by Mass Observation in a Blackpool pub. 'It's a war of nerves', said one drinker to another. 'Nerves my arse,' was the reply. 'It's boring me bloody well stiff. No football neither.' The pubs and churches stayed open when most other public gathering places were closed but their morale boosting resources were not enough to prevent the 'war of nerves' tailing off into a 'war of yawns'. For Churchill (who, as First Lord of the Admiralty, made almost the only warlike sounds from the Government benches) this was a period of 'pretended war' in the twilight,

although there was nothing to pretend about in the sinking of the *Athenia*, torpedoed off the Hebrides, or the mining of the Dutch ship, the *Simon Bolivar*, or, for that matter, in most of the early episodes of the long-drawn-out and cruel war at sea.

Churchill, as First Lord, did not like the way shipping losses were announced . . . and he liked even less the reporting of the Norwegian campaign before the *Sitzkrieg* ended in the west and the Germans struck in Holland and Belgium. Indeed how to describe or not to describe seemed the real question in the phoney war, not how to act or not to act, and Tommy Handley's Ministry of Aggravation and Mysteries was always ready to give unwanted advice. The French too had their own line with its entrenchments described appropriately by Harold Nicolson (whose November Penguin Special *Why Britain is at War* soon sold a hundred thousand copies) as 'like the BBC buried in a mountain'. At home the House of Commons itself seemed to him to set the low key and he described his sense of shame when newly-arrived Dominion representatives came to hear debates in the Commons Gallery. 'They had come expecting to find the Mother of Parliaments armed like Britannia. They merely saw an old lady dozing over her knitting, while her husband read the paper aloud.'

Most people, however, were conscious not of shame but of a feeling of anti-climax. Mollie Panter-Downes, the *New Yorker*'s London correspondent, described the public as 'feeling like a little boy who stuffs his fingers in his ears on the fourth of July, only to discover that the cannon cracker has not gone off after all'. People were prepared for bombs, not boredom, just as the Government, having prepared for panic, could not cope with anti-climax. 'The British people,' wrote Sir Samuel Hoare, 'was ready to accept great sacrifices but not minor irritations.' It was not yet time for the sacrifices and in the meantime the irritations provided much that was funny . . . in both senses of the word.

What was funny/peculiar was what Harold Macmillan called 'the smell of peace in the air' . . . the old dirty washing again. Lloyds were laying odds in late October 1939 that the war would be over by December. Even the King in his Christmas

broadcast included the sentences, 'We cannot tell what it [the new year] will bring. If it brings peace, how happy we shall all be.' There was some toughening up early in the new year, but the smell of peace – sickly not sweet – never disappeared from the air. The Russian invasion of Finland in November 1939, and the real winter war in the north which followed, even made some British people – not only the Chamberlainites, who had always hated communism – wonder whether they were fighting the right enemy. Eventually Hitler's invasion of Norway was to provide the answer and make the phoney war a real one, but in those winter months of 1939–40 Sir Robert Bruce Lockhart reported that wherever he went he heard the same remark, 'The British people will win the war in spite of the Government.'

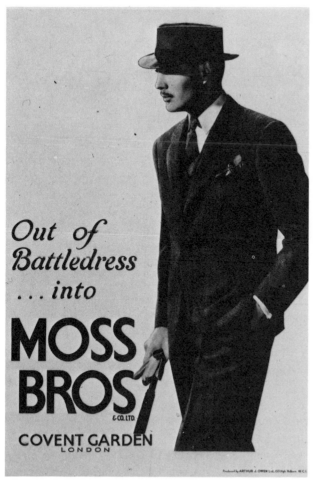

Out of Battledress . . . into

MOSS BROS & CO. LTD.

COVENT GARDEN LONDON

Produced by ARTHUR J. OWEN Ltd, 155 High Holborn, W.C.1.

HOUSE OF COMMONS

Secret Session

Chamberlain: "No admittance! All seats reserved for the ruling class and their friends"

Yet there was much to laugh at too. This kind of funniness   ha-ha – was also bound up with the strange blend of 'normal' and 'abnormal'. It was funny to read in the *Daily Telegraph* in September 1939 of a woman carrying a gas mask 'in a satchel of violet velvet adorned with artificial roses', or in *The Times*, in December, an advertisement suggesting that readers might stock up with 'nature's syren, the pheasant', guaranteed to give 'audible warning of bombs long before the human ear can detect them'. Christmas itself, if not a spree, was still a guzzle. This time *The Economist* was good reading. Its front pages set out an analysis of the conflicting advice on whether to save or spend from Oliver Stanley at the Board of Trade and Kingsley Wood at the Exchequer (the former in the role of Father Christmas), and its back page carried three full advertisements for Australian wines, French cheese and trips to the French colonies, especially Algeria. Nothing could quite

South Wales, Hodson saw shipyards and factories working night and day to produce ships and munitions. 'Not since 1917 or 1918 has this area [Clydeside] been so full of work. Between the last war and this it has not been equalled. What a terrible fact that is!'

COUNTY BOROUGH OF SOUTHAMPTON.
Local Invasion Committee

A Local Invasion Committee has been set up in order to deal with invasion conditions.

DURING THE PRESENT PERIOD the Committee is engaged in making preparations to deal with the local problems which will arise in invasion such as :—

1. Organisation of civilian labour to assist the military in preparing defence works, digging trenches, clearing roads, etc.
2. Care of wounded.
3. Housing and sheltering the homeless.
4. Emergency cooking and feeding.
5. Emergency water supplies.
6. Messenger Service.

IF INVASION COMES the Committee will direct its action :

(a) to meet the requirements of the military,
(b) to attend to the needs of the civil population.

live up to this in the late winter and the early spring of 1940, but it was funny then to read a letter in a Leicestershire parish magazine from a clergyman who wondered whether women ARP workers really did need to wear trousers. It was even funny when the phoney war was over, and one old lady was heard to say, 'There's this to be said for the Blitz – it does take your mind off the blackout.'

For some people the phoney war meant neither fun nor frustration. When J. L. Hodson visited Tyneside in early April 1940 he asked a motor driver what struck him as the biggest change since the war. He said, 'Seeing six times as many people as usual coming out of the factories.' At Jarrow Hodson saw men of sixty and seventy going off to work again after years of unemployment. 'The war has given them a fresh lease of work . . . There's a sense in which Hitler has given to the country a unity it didn't possess.' All over the previously depressed areas, Clydeside, Tyneside and Teeside,

'Terrible' the implications may have been but the facts of the phoney war were not. Bombs did not fall; depressed areas were now prosperous; people grew more sociable as they shared the inconveniences of the blackout, evacuation and rationing. The irony of the employment situation, the fun, the frustration – all were different aspects of the same psychological fact; the failure of the war to conform to people's expectations of action and attack. It had even started with a phoney air raid warning – a false alarm. Cities had been destroyed before September 1939 as Warsaw was now being destroyed. The stage was set for an intensive and early attack by Germany. But London and Paris and Berlin were safe from everything but leaflets and fairly safe from them. Air Vice Marshall 'Bomber' Harris later assessed the effectiveness of the leaflet raids: 'My personal view is that the only thing achieved was largely to supply the Continent's requirements of toilet paper for the five long years of war.' The feebleness of the leaflet campaign gave rise to a whole string of jokes about 'Mein Pamph' and imaginary conversations between flying officers:

'Why are you back so early from the raid?'
'I dropped my leaflets in bundles; that was right, wasn't it?'
'Good God! You might have hurt somebody.'

But leaflet-dropping and occasional reconnaissance flights over the Siegfried Line were no substitute for real action in the air. Soldiers too had professional as well as psychological reasons for wanting the real war on the Western Front to begin and one typical phoney war joke was that the troops were knitting comforts for the civilians. 'What we want is action,' an infantryman told J. L. Hodson in France in December 1939. 'He [the soldier] wants conviction that what he is being asked to do is the finest way of defeating the enemy.' The action did not come until May 1940, and it came then so thick and fast and full of so many terrifying surprises that the moods of the phoney war disappeared overnight. Kingsley Martin, editor of the *New Statesman*, a somewhat unlikely witness to martial attitudes, reported on 8 June 1940 that 'life has become much more tolerable as the real danger has appeared'.

The 'real dangers' in France were all too apparent after the fall of Holland and Belgium: subversion by the Fifth Column; political intrigue at the centre; shortage of aircraft; the collapse of armies; refugees on the roads. As the Siegfried Line (and the Maginot Line after it) receded into the distance, the dirty washing continued to pile up. The strangeness of the 'strange defeat' was more sinister than the funniness of the phoney war.

There was no Siegfried Line in England when the troops returned from France in their little boats. But there was the sea lapping against the white cliffs of Dover. It had served as an outlet for centuries and at first did not seem like a barrier. But it was, even when it was not set on fire. England was not invaded, although the threat of invasion made everyone draw deep on the rich reserves of history – Spaniards, not Germans, and Drake before

Churchill. Dunkirk itself, as Priestley put it in one of his first broadcasts, became an immediate epic. 'Our great-grandchildren,' he said, 'when they learn how we began this war by snatching glory out of defeat, and then swept on to victory, may also learn how the little holiday steamers made an excursion to hell and came back glorious.'

At a time when no one in England was any longer singing 'We're gonna hang out the washing on the Siegfried Line', A. P. Herbert penned a new song in June 1940 – this time with no music – which was in its way as defiant as Priestley's prose:

Dear Uncle Sam, I seem to remember
(Was it October or was it November?)
Somebody called it a phoney war –
Somebody said it was rather a bore . . .

Dear Uncle Sam, do you still think, brother,
One bit of Europe's as bad as another?
Possibly Sam, but forgive us, do,
For now you're a corner of Europe too.

They were good words, but they were not quite right. The King caught the new mood even better,

" Nearly eight months this war's been on—and what have we got to show for it?"

as he had caught the Christmas mood. In a letter to his mother he wrote, 'Personally I feel happier now that we have no allies to be polite to and to pamper.' The Spitfires were ready (planned in the early years of rearmament). The air raid wardens had been drilling for months to be well prepared. The Local Defence Volunteers (not yet the Home Guard) were 'standing to'. Winston Churchill was Prime Minister and the country, to quote his phrase, had at last 'found its soul'.

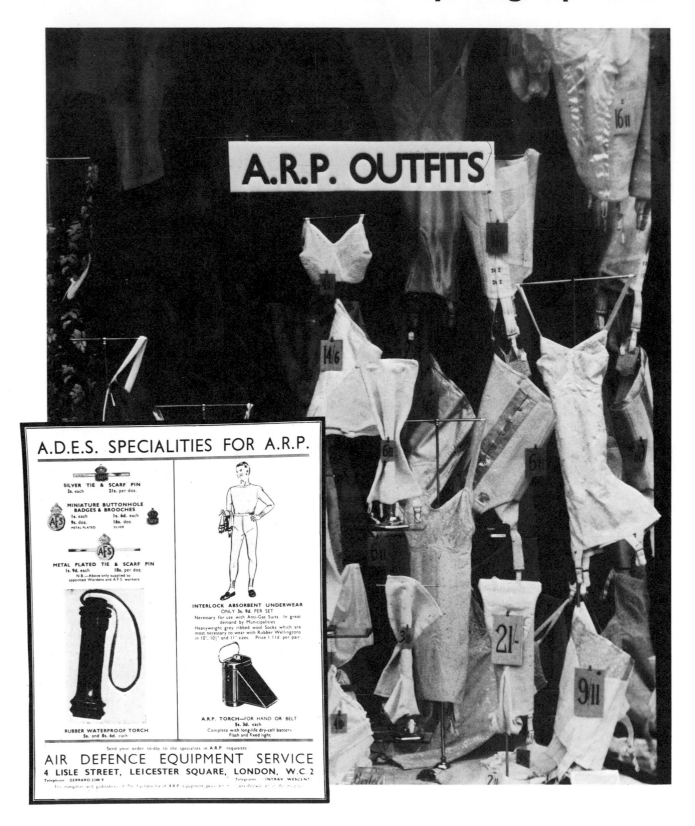

A.R.P. OUTFITS

A.D.E.S. SPECIALITIES FOR A.R.P.

SILVER TIE & SCARF PIN
2s. each   21s. per doz.

MINIATURE BUTTONHOLE
BADGES & BROOCHES
1s. each   1s. 6d. each
9s. doz.   16s. doz.
METAL PLATED   SILVER

METAL PLATED TIE & SCARF PIN
1s. 9d. each   18s. per doz.
N.B.—Above only supplied to
appointed Wardens and A.F.S. workers

INTERLOCK ABSORBENT UNDERWEAR
ONLY 3s. 9d. PER SET
Necessary for use with Anti-Gas Suits. In great
demand by Municipalities
Heavyweight grey ribbed wool Socks which are
most necessary to wear with Rubber Wellingtons
in 10", 10½" and 11" sizes.   Price 1 11d. per pair.

RUBBER WATERPROOF TORCH
5s. and 8s. 6d. each

A.R.P. TORCH—FOR HAND OR BELT
5s. 3d. each.
Complete with long-life dry-cell battery
Flash and fixed light

Send your order to-day to the specialists in A.R.P. requisites

AIR DEFENCE EQUIPMENT SERVICE
4 LISLE STREET, LEICESTER SQUARE, LONDON, W.C.2
Telephone GERRARD 2148 9   Telegrams   INTRAV WESCENT

. but nothing is likely' (Quoted in *New Statesman*, October 1939)

Contemporary definition of ARP:
'Angling Round Pubs.'

'Those who take part in BBC variety programmes are now told they may use any term they like for the Nazi Government. Hitherto they have been restricted to the more polite descriptions.'(*News Chronicle*, 30 September 1939)

UNDER MY HELMET
Big-helmet Wilkie they call me,
 Big-helmet Wilkie, that's me:
Now that they've made me a warden
 I get my torch batt'ries free!

Once, at the sound of a warning,
 A blonde cried, 'Shelter me, please!'
Then said, 'That isn't a rattle;
 'Blimey — it's your knocking knees!'

  Big-helmet Wilkie they call me,
   Wilkie the Warden, that's me!
(*The ARP and AFS Magazine*, early 1940)

In a street of a certain character an ARP Warden noticed a faulty blackout. He said to the woman who answered his knock: 'There's a chink in that room up there.' 'No', she said, 'it's not a Chink: it's a Japanese gentleman.' (September 1940)

The ARP inspired many parodies from 'Alice in Arpland' to a Biblical 'Book of Arp' by Norman Tiptaft, Birmingham's Civil Defence boss: '. . . and Jonand (Sir John Anderson, Home Secretary) spake:

"Say thus to the people. Ye have been entreated to join Arp and to train with them that are at the Stations of Auxiliary Fire and at the Posts of the Wardens of First Aid." '

'There are no plums on this job:

"We'll give her another ten minutes, and then warn her."

"Don't be alarmed. There is no fire—we're only practising."

" Put that light out ! "

PATRIOTIC DOWN TO THE PANTEES!

'These slick little pantees, beautifully embroidered with the "Washing on the Siegfried Line", and the slogan, "England Expects . . ." might come in the category of "improperganda", but as a gift for any lingerie drawer they're certain of a rapturous welcome.'
(Advertisement in *Birmingham Post*, December 1939)

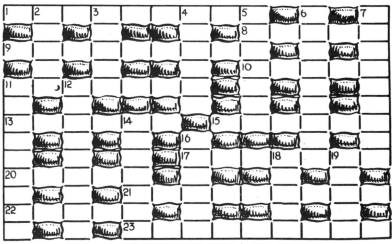

A.R.P. CROSSWORD PUZZLE NO. 1

46

. if it's civil?' (Saying attributed to Mae West)

Henry Ellison.

Age 7.

Item from an autumn 1939 gardening catalogue (to add to the mosaics): 'Collections for covering mounds of air raid shelters: berberis, cotoneaster, cydonia, etc.'

. Be wise and do the job now'

(From Civil Defence leaflet, Ministry of Home Security, 1939)

The day war broke out these Londoners took their canary down the dug-out when the first siren of the war sounded (*below left*).

'After building "the finest air raid shelter in the country" at a cost of £24,000 in the garden of her mansion overlooking Torbay, Mrs Ella Marion Rowcroft, 81-year-old millionairess, has died without using it . . . A lift took us more than thirty feet down below the ground into a fifty-yard-long corridor with rooms opening out on each side . . . Then we went into the bedroom the millionairess had planned for herself . . . At the head of the bed was a bronze plate with the words: "Angels are watching overhead. Sleep sweetly, then. Good night".' (*Daily Express*, March 1941)

By summer 1941 one American journalist noted that 'there was a greater danger of being hit by a vegetable marrow falling off the roof of an air raid shelter than of being struck by a bomb'.

IMPORTANT!
NO. OF PERSONS SLEEPING IN THIS HOUSE

DOG / CAT
(Cross out whichever is inapplicable)

ALSO **IN HOUSE HIS BED IS**

(State location of bed as exactly as possible.)

Issued by
The National Canine
Defence League,
Victoria Station House,
S.W.1.

The Royal Society for the
Prevention of Cruelty
to Animals,
105, Jermyn Street, S.W.1.

'Send your pets to the country if you can.

If you cannot, remember that your dog will not be allowed to go into a public air raid shelter with you.

So don't take him shopping with you.

Take him for walks near home, so that you can get back quickly.

When you take him into your own shelter with you, put him on a lead.

If you can get a muzzle for him, you should do so, because he may get hysterical during raids.

Put some cotton wool in his ears.

Ask your chemist to mix a dose of bromide all ready for you to give him when a raid starts.

Don't worry about your cats.

Cats can take care of themselves far better than you can. Your cat will probably meet you when you get into the shelter.'
(From *Hints on Household ARP*, a 1939 broadcast)

By January 1940 most people had stopped carrying gas masks and in the Will Hay film *The Goose Steps Out* (1942) a would-be German spy was taught that if he wanted to be accepted as a true Englishman he must avoid at all costs carrying a gas mask. (*Below*) Decontamination exercise.

your gas mask will take care of you' (ARP slogan)

ALAS. POOR GHOST

'All gas and gaiters' might have been the title of this painting by E. Dunbar (*left*), officially commissioned to demonstrate an ARP warden's complete gas-proof suit (never to be needed).

'Are the little ones used to seeing you in YOUR mask? Make a game of it, calling it 'Mummy's Funny Face,' or something of the kind; then if the time comes when you *really* have to wear it, you won't be a terrifying apparition to the child.' (From a 1939 broadcast *The Care of Children in Wartime*)

Little girl to mother who has been pretending that her 'Mickey Mouse' child's gas mask is a new game: 'It's all right, Mummy. I know what it is. It's a gas mask, and we put it on when they bomb us.'

" You first put your chin in it."

'A couple of real air raids is what we want'

(Mass Observation Report, early 1940)

(*Above*) *A Balloon Site, Coventry* by
Laura Knight.
Dear old lady: If those Germans think
they can frighten me by sitting up in
those balloons all the time, they're very
much mistaken.

Many barrage balloons were made by
the girls at Littlewoods of Liverpool,
the football pool firm. At Christmas 1939
there were even toy barrage balloons
on sale and Christmas cards showing
Santa Claus being shot down by anti-
aircraft guns.

'The object of the balloon barrage is
mainly to force attacking aircraft to
heights at which accurate bombing is
impossible, and where the use of machine
guns upon a civilian population is
impracticable.' (Article in *ARP and AFS
Review*, autumn 1939)

'It puts you in mind of a big whale'

(*Mass Observation Report* on attitudes to barrage balloons)

An early wartime feature film, *The Lion has Wings*, showed the *Luftwaffe* turning back in terror at the sight of Britain's massed balloon barrage. (*Below*) *Anti-Aircraft Site* by Kenneth Rowntree, 1940.

(*Left*) The one that got away . . .This barrage balloon broke away from its moorings and came to rest in the Barrack Street district of Leeds in May 1940.

'Bloody Marvellous'

(Headline to *Daily Mirror* editorial after Dunkirk)

(*Right*) The 'valiant little ships return to Dover', painting by Muirhead Bone.

Dunkirk, May 1940, came nine months after the war had started. Despite a colossal military defeat, the newsreels still put an optimistic gloss on it. NEWSREEL: 'Now, after a re-issue of kit and a wash, they're anxious to get back and have another go: "Well, now that I'm back in Blighty for a few days, get kitted, I'll be out there and smack them up again." The story of Dunkirk has brought home to us at last the grim reality of this war. With the example of these men ever before us, we must now put aside every thought save one, to work for victory.'

'Wars are not won by evacuations'

(Churchill to the House of Commons, 4 June 1940)

'So long as the English tongue survives, the word Dunkirk will be spoken with reverence. For in that harbour, in such a hell as never blazed on earth before, at the end of a lost battle, the rags and blemishes that have hidden the soul of Democracy fell away. There, beaten but unconquered in shining splendour she faced the enemy. This shining thing in the souls of free men Hitler cannot command or attain or conquer . . . It is the great tradition of Democracy. It is the future. It is Victory.' (*New York Times*, 1 June 1940)

Returning troops, many of them wounded (*left*), had a warm welcome. (*Opposite below*) Locals of Headcorn, Kent, where troop trains stopped for refreshments, cut up bread and butter day and night for a week.

CIGARETTES are always welcomed BY THE TROOPS !

'Our chaps will deal with them'

GENERALS ALL

'Mr Bartlett (Independent, Bridgwater) asked Mr Eden if he was aware that in one LDV company there were six different generals all dressed up as generals.' (House of Commons report, July 1940) (The Home Guard, renamed by Churchill himself, was originally the LDV or Local Defence Volunteers.)

Last night a Stand-To was ordered. Thirty
    men of us here
Came out to guard the star-lit village – my
    men who wear
Unwitting the seasons' beauty, the received
    truth of the spade –
Roadmen, farm labourers, masons, turned
    to another trade.

A dog barked over the fields, the candle
    stars put a sheen
On the rifles ready, the sandbags fronded
    with evergreen:
The dawn wind blew, the stars winked out
    on the posts where we lay,
The order came, Stand Down, and thirty
    went away.
(From *Stand-To* by Cecil Day-Lewis,
September 1940)

'Their rights were simple, namely nil'

(Historian of a Yorkshire Home Guard Battalion on the Women's Home Defence)

2nd Bb CLARINET

LIVERPOOL BRASS BAND (& MILITARY) JOURNAL
PUBLISHED BY WRIGHT & ROUND 34, ERSKINE STREET, LIVERPOOL

HOME GUARD

QUICK MARCH

G. SOUTHWELL

*There's a Home Guard Sentry at the end
of Lover's Lane
So it's no place for lovers anymore . . .
And when you say 'Dear Heart, will you be
mine?'
Someone answers 'Friend, advance and give
the countersign.'*
(Popular song of 1943)

'. . . . they were to accompany the warriors into battle but were denied the protection of the steel helmet, service respirator . . . and hardly-won great-coat. They were not to be taught anything of a military nature . . .'
(Wartime description of the Women's Home Defence, *below*, a member.)

(*Below left*) Rifle Drill for the House of Commons LDV Corps.

'Wir fahren gegen Engelland'

(German popular song, summer 1940)

Means of hindering Nazi troop-carriers from crash landing. (*Illustrated London News*, summer 1940)

'He is coming!' 'He is coming!'

(Hitler, of himself and his plans to invade Britain) (*Sports Palace* speech, 4 September 1940)

Issued on behalf of the **Ministry of War Transport**

IMMOBILISATION OF VEHICLES

IN THE EVENT OF INVASION

Every owner of a motor vehicle should be ready, in the event of invasion, to immobilise his car, cycle or lorry the moment the order is given. Failure to act promptly would give the enemy the chance to provide himself with transport.

It is important that owners of vehicles should understand now what they have to do, and satisfy themselves that they can carry out the order at any time without delay.

With a view to helping them, the Ministry of Transport gives the following information and advice on what they must do when informed by the Police or through the Civil Defence services that immobilisation of vehicles has been ordered in their area:

Petrol Vehicles

Remove distributor head and leads, and empty the tank or remove the carburettor.

Diesel-Engined Vehicles

Remove the injection pump and connection.

HIDE THE PARTS REMOVED WELL AWAY FROM THE VEHICLE

OPERATION SEA LION

'On 1 and 2 September, "the invasion of England" was filmed for the German newsreels in the harbour of Antwerp, with the bathing beach of St Anne serving to represent the shores of Albion.

Here, for two days, invasion barges drew in to the shore and men leapt into the shallow water as light tanks and motor-cycles rolled from the concrete decks to the sandy beach, firing as they went. One of the men in charge explained to me the reason: "You see," he said, "when we invade England it will be at night, or very early in the morning, and there won't be enough light to photograph it. Since this will be the decisive event of the war, it must be covered for the newsreel — so we're staging it here, exactly as it will be done later on the English coast".' (Lars Moen)

'Do not give any German anything. Do not tell him anything. Hide your food and your bicycles. Hide your maps . . . Think always of your country before you think of yourself.' (From *If the Invader Comes*, public information leaflet, June 1940)

Teacher: 'Oh to be in England!' Now boys and girls, can anyone tell me who said that?
Cockney pupil: 'itler!

'...a state of complete panic...

(German propaganda for Britain)

I was playing golf when the Germans landed;
All our ships had gone away and all our men were stranded;
And the thought of England's shame
Nearly put me off my game.
(Lyric of First World War song, revived in 1940)

'For the second week in succession the Crown Office and the College of Arms have had to work at top speed in the preparation of patents of peerages.'
(News item in *Daily Telegraph*, June 1940)

Edward Ardizzone painted this untroubled scene (*below*) on Bournemouth beach in the early summer of 1940 – just before the barbed wire went up on Britain's beaches, and before the leaflets of Hitler's *Reichstag* speech, *A Last Appeal to Reason*, fluttered down on the British countryside.

"*... meanwhile, in Britain, the entire population, faced by the threat of invasion, has been flung into a state of complete panic ...*"

THERE'LL ALWAYS BE AN ENGLAND

'VERY WELL, ALONE'

There'll always be an England
And England shall be free
If England means as much to you
As England means to me.

Britain found its soul – so it was said – during the 'Battle of Britain', a battle that was named before it began. On 18 June 1940 Churchill, still new to the challenge of power, remarked succinctly that what General Weygand had called the Battle of France was over. 'I expect,' he went on, 'that the Battle of Britain is about to begin. Upon this battle depends the survival of Christian civilization.'

This was not the first time such a phrase had been used, but the battle itself – very different from all battles for national survival before, including the Battle of France – was a battle in the skies, a battle of the few to save the many. Hitler's *Adlertag* (Eagle Day) on 13 August was the beginning of an experience very different from that which Hitler – or Goering – had anticipated. What started with boasts on the German side ended with pride on the British.

The fighter pilots, young, brave and alone, became symbols of Britain herself, now standing alone. The skies of Kent and Sussex were the scene of the first British 'battlefield' since Culloden and thousands of spectators watched in terror, excitement and admiration the critical dog-fights in progress above them. Newspaper placards bore scrawled 'scores' like 167 for 33 as if the battle was a new game.

The pilots themselves disliked references to glory and heroism – even when they daily risked their lives in air battles. Contrasting sharply with Churchill's speeches – or Priestley's – some of the liveliest slang of the war was the RAF language of understatement. The diffidence, the throwaway line, the irony – all were part of the legend. The RAF man flew a 'kite', put it away in 'a shed', often slept in 'an iron lung' (a Nissen Hut). He referred to the dropping of bombs as 'leaving visiting cards', 'laying eggs' or 'distributing cookies', and when he went on operations 'over the ditch' he hoped he would not 'go for a Burton', 'write himself off' or,

MAY THE MANY OWE MUCH TO *THESE* FEW

in some sense, 'have had it'. It was a special language designed to be exclusive but, like the best slang, was soon to be heard everywhere.

The most famous pilot of all, Richard Hillary, himself a symbol of a type, even of a generation, explained the fascination of the life in his own language: 'In a Spitfire we're back to war as it ought to be – if you can talk about war as it ought to be. Back to individual combat, to self-reliance, total responsibility for one's fate', everything, in fact, that the First World War had *not* been for the fighting man.

The battle was followed by the Blitz (which started even before it had ended). No longer was it the destiny of single individuals in combat which was at stake, but the fate of millions in the cities.

The Blitz was folk lore before it became history, as great a source of legends as the battle. The noise of the bombs and the sirens has died away, but the recorded siren still serves as a signal and the songs survive and so do the pictures. Just after the war General Sir Frederick Pile, who had been General Officer-in-Charge of the Anti-Aircraft Command, came upon a pair of ear-plugs hanging on a wall in a silversmith's attic near his office. There was a notice under them:

ANTIQUES OF THE FUTURE
Issued by the Ministry of Home Security to Londoners (and never used) so that we should not hear our guns, which were music.

Even before the Blitz was folk lore it had been prophecy. A novel published in 1931, *The Gas War of 1940*, was wrong about the gas but it prophesied a German *Blitzkrieg* to start in September 1939 and then the English kind of *Blitz* (note how we appropriated that and another German term, the Siegfried Line).

And then in a moment [the author wrote] the lights of London vanished as if blotted out by a gigantic extinguisher. And in the dark streets, the burned and wounded, bewildered and panic-stricken, fought and struggled like beasts scrambling over the dead and dying alike until they fell and were in turn trodden underfoot by the ever-increasing multitudes about them.

This prophecy was false, although it needed new myths to demolish it. The cost of the 'Blitz' was enormous – in property even more than in lives – but instead of being torn apart like beasts, the victims of the Blitz discovered a new solidarity. There was little panic, even little absenteeism. It did not need a Ministry of Information – or a Churchill – to proclaim to the world 'Britain can take it'. Mark Benney, working in an aircraft factory says that people still went to work after a night of horror 'in part because we all felt that the raids give an added importance to our work, but much more because we knew that if we didn't turn up our mates would be worrying'. Innumerable stories illustrating British imperturbability were in circulation. Ernestine Carter, at the time working at the Ministry of Information, tells a true story about her husband's tailor, Hawes, of Hawes and Curtis in Jermyn Street whose shop was bombed. The day after Mr Hawes, standing outside the debris, immaculately dressed in a dove-grey suit, grey suède shoes, grey hat, a button-hole, walking stick and gloves, smoking a cigarette in an amber holder, is approached by two customers, one a Mr French, a theatrical producer.

Hawes: Good morning, Mr French. Nice day.
French: Morning, Hawes. You're looking well. This is Colonel Egerton.
Hawes: How do you do, Colonel. Very interesting news from East Africa this morning. Tell me, Mr French, how is your new show coming along? I've been watching the theatrical prospects with much interest.
French: Well, we open next month. I'll send you a couple of stalls, of course, as usual.
Hawes: Extremely good of you. I must say there are few things I enjoy more than a first night. And now, gentlemen, if you'll just step this way, I'd like to show you the fucking mess they've made of my shop.

The Germans on another occasion, mistaking Hardwicke Hall where the Dowager Duchess of Devonshire was living for a munitions factory, dropped a stick of bombs which fortunately all landed in the avenue. Her Grace summoned the old butler whom she had taken with her from Chatsworth. 'Tell me, Parkinson, what was it like?' she asked. After a pause Parkinson replied. 'Your Grace, I cannot recall anything so spectacular since Lord Hartington's coming of age.'

The Germans, meanwhile, were putting a different interpretation on British imperturbability – as this extract from the *Schwarze Korps*, the organ of Hitler's Black Guards, in October 1940 shows:

Londoners' ability to carry on under continuous bombing amid the seething wreckage and raging planes, without a roof over their heads, without sleep, and with only the most slender food supplies, is not due to the British ability to 'take it' or to their proverbial toughness.

Rather England approaches death with sensual pleasure and smacks its lips. Psychopaths know of such cases where the pleasure of destruction is paralleled by the pleasure of self-destruction. There lies the solution of British toughness and endurance.

Another myth of the Blitz was that it levelled classes of society as well as buildings, and it was certainly true, to cite the classic example, that the bombing of Buckingham Palace emphasized the extent to which the King and Queen were sharing the same dangers as their East End subjects. Harold Nicolson quoted in his diary a comment of the Liberal politician Clement Davies after the bombing of Buckingham Palace (a comment fortunately not overheard by Haw-Haw):

If only the Germans had had the sense not to bomb West of London Bridge there might have been a revolution in this country. As it is, they have smashed about Bond Street and Park Lane and readjusted the balance.

Such feelings of vague national solidarity between Ed Murrow's 'little people' and the 'Big Ones' were perfectly compatible with individual displays of continuing class snobbery. At one end of the social scale James Agate reported a conversation overheard at the Ritz shortly after a bad night of bombing: 'I'm not a snob, but I thank heaven there are plenty of common people to clear up the mess.' At the other end of the scale F. Tennyson Jesse reported the experience of a friend on stretcher-duty:

She was working to help dig out a very large woman of the 'char' class who was wedged in the remains of a poor little house with an unexploded time bomb about twenty yards away. She kept on repeating 'I don't want you young ladies to get hurt on account of me. You leave me alone, I'll be all right.'

The Blitz began on 7 September, while there was still a very real fear of invasion too. And it could not be demonstrated then that the German decision to switch the Battle of Britain from the aerodromes to the cities was an intimation that the invasion would never come. What did become plain – and could be said loudly as well as openly –

in the autumn and winter of 1940–1 was how different the Second World War was proving from the First. Then there had been an enormous psychological gulf between the soldiers in the trenches and those they had left behind in London. Now London – and the other great cities – were in the front line. In September 1940 John Balderstier, a friend of F. Tennyson Jesse, reported that at a dinner in the British Embassy in Washington an American was worrying about the morale of civilians in London, and an Englishwoman turned to him and said very simply: 'There are no civilians in London.' For fifty-seven consecutive nights London was bombed, and it was often bombed in the daytime too. (By 14 November the *Luftwaffe* had lost so many aircraft and men that they concentrated on night operations only, and so continued until mid-1941 when the great Blitz ended and Hitler transferred his attention to the Russian front.)

The toll was heavy. During the four months from 7 September 1940 to New Year's Day 1941 13,339 people in London were killed and 17,937 severely injured. And the worst night was yet to come. On May 10/11 1941 1436 people were killed and 1752 injured. Most of them left no epitaphs, but there was no shortage of prayers, if only the simplest prayer of all, 'Please God don't let them stop here.'

While songs, cartoons and music-hall jokes kept horror submerged – a sense of humour was said to be the British 'secret weapon' – George Orwell rationalized about what was happening in Britain.

Highly civilized human beings are flying overhead, trying to kill me . . . Most of them, I have no doubt, are kindly, law-abiding men who would never dream of committing murder in private life. On the other hand, if one of them succeeds in blowing me to pieces with a well-placed bomb, he will never sleep any the worse for it.

George Orwell was not blown to pieces, but many bomb victims were, and one of the grimmest tasks for which the ARP was responsible was helping to piece bodies together in preparation for burial. One VAD (Voluntary Aid Detachment) was chosen for the work, despite her youth, because she had studied anatomy at the Slade. 'It was a very difficult task,' she wrote. 'There were so many pieces missing and, as one of the mortuary attendants said, "proper jigsaw puzzle, ain't it, Miss?"'

The fires had turned the city-scape of London into a hell on the terrible night of 29 December 1940, when the city was devastated, and on many other nights – as the blackout was lit up by the enemy. Fire, indeed, was one of the most violent of all the realities of the war: F. Tennyson Jesse and H. M. Harwood called their book of collected letters, written to America from July 1940 to June 1941 (published in 1942), *While London Burns*, and Constantine Fitzgibbon calls his superb account of the Blitz *London's Burning*. Coventry, more ravaged even than London, which was too big to destroy, chose a phoenix as its symbol of recovery.

London was never the only city target. The destruction of Coventry on the night of 14 November – a 'massacre' which was compared with that of Rotterdam and Warsaw – was followed by a switch of the German attack to the Midlands, and Birmingham was attacked by 350 German bombs five days later. There were many other attacks in 1941 as well as in 1940 – the last raid on Birmingham, for example, did not come until April 1943 – and there were cities and towns in other parts of Britain also which were regularly battered – Southampton, Bristol, Hull, Plymouth. All had their own tales to tell - and their own pictures of death and destruction, although there were few pictures more magnificent than than of St Paul's which stood out, according to one contemporary observer, 'last, loneliest, loveliest, apart . . . in a desolation comparable to that of Ypres'. It is a picture that everyone has come to know.

All the pictures, familiar or unfamiliar, still catch the immediacy of the Blitz, and if not every picture still tells a story, there are many stories with no pictures to accompany them. This was the folk lore – tales of what had happened (or not happened) the night before (the 'bomb' story became the latest new way to bore your friends and acquaintances); of laughter in the shelter – or

even in the debris – there is a myth that every Cockney ever dug out of rubble had a wise-crack on his or her lips; of tears; of heroes without names; of firemen as much as fires. Even Goebbels went on to pay his own wartime tribute to London. In December 1940, weeks after Hitler had called off the threatened invasion, he made it clear that there would be no early end to the war. Years later, in August 1943, when Berlin was itself under the heavy attack that he and Goering had told Germans would never come, he wrote an article in tones very different from the German propaganda of 1940:

What the English stuck out in the autumn, and for which a few of us admired them, that we have to stick out now. I reject indignantly the enemy allegation that the Berliners have weaker nerves than the Londoners. This is out of the question.

By then far more was 'out of the question' though London was still to suffer its last air attack from VIs and V2s (portents of the future). The Blitz was already history, like the Christmas of 1940, so very different from the Christmas of 1939. 'This is not a Merry Christmas in London,' Ed Murrow noted on 24 December 1940. 'I heard that phrase only twice in the last three days.'

'We shall defend our island home . . .'

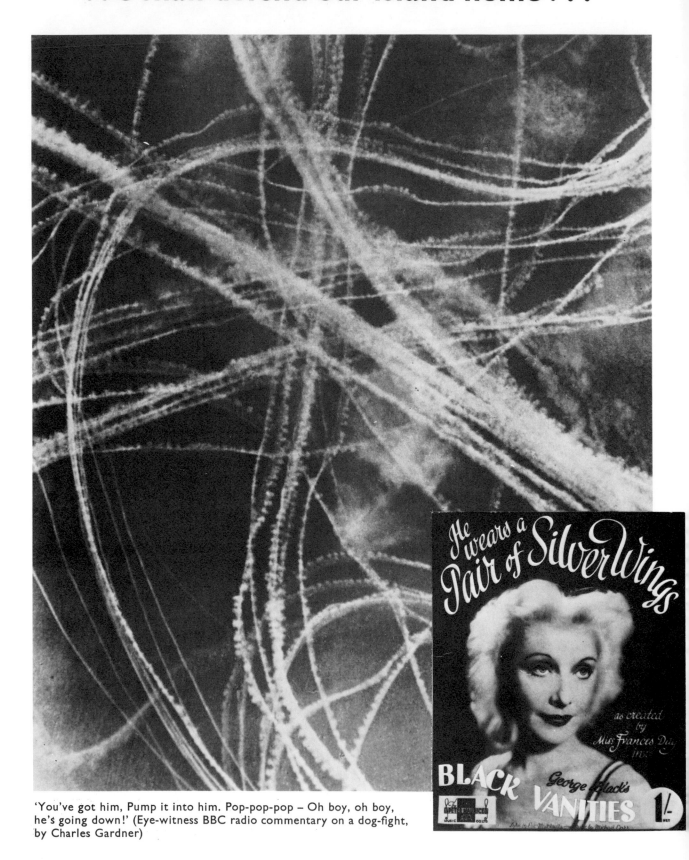

'You've got him, Pump it into him. Pop-pop-pop – Oh boy, oh boy, he's going down!' (Eye-witness BBC radio commentary on a dog-fight, by Charles Gardner)

'We shall fight . . . in the air'

(Churchill, June 1940)

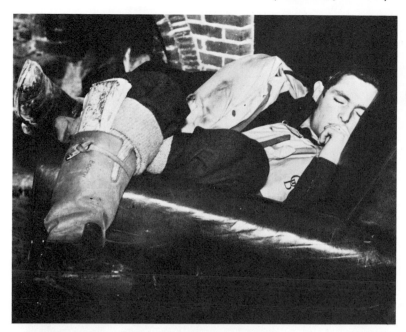

These are the boys of whom we said
'They are not what their fathers were;
They have no heart, and little head;
They slouch, and do not cut their hair'.

Yet these like falcons live and die;
These every night have new renown;
And while we heave a single sigh
They shoot a brace of bombers down.
(A. P. Herbert, 28 July 1940)

At Gravesend one of 'the Few' (*above left*) snatches a rest. Some Battle of Britain pilots called their uniforms 'sleeping suits' because they were never out of them, standing-to day and night, to take the air at five minutes' notice.

Schoolchildren in 'Hell's Corner' (Kent) watch a dogfight (*left*). The throb and whine of aircraft engines, crashed enemy aircraft (fair game for souvenir-hunters) and skies criss-crossed with vapour trails (*opposite left*) were part of life in August and September 1940.

Recruiting Sergeant: What makes you think you can handle a Spitfire?
Accordionist: I should be able to . . . I've been married to one for ten years.

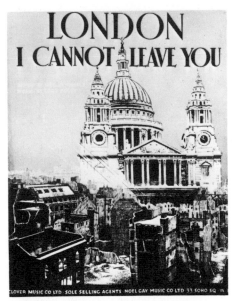

LONDON
I CANNOT LEAVE YOU

COVER MUSIC CO LTD · SOLE SELLING AGENTS NOEL GAY MUSIC CO LTD 33 SOHO SQ W

'You know, mate, I ain't a religious
bloke – I never go to church, and I don't
pray or anything. But I should hate to
see dear old St Paul's hurt or damaged.
Somehow – you know what I mean,
mate – somehow – well, blast it all, it's
London, ain't it?' (City printer overheard
by Guy Eden, quoted in *Portrait of
Churchill*)

St Paul's survived relatively unscathed –
a symbol of Britain's own survival –
amidst acres of desolate waste. One
bomb did explode through the roof.
'This grandiose litter had the majesty
of a Piranesi; one thought of Gibbon and
not of Wren,' wrote James Pope-
Hennessy after a tour of the damage.
The *Architectural Review*, arguing in 1944
for the preservation of the ruins of some
city churches, wrote, 'The devastation
of war has given us an opportunity
which will never come again. If we do
not make the City of London worth the
spirit of those who fought the Battle of
Britain, posterity will rise and curse us
for unimaginative fools.'

'London property of every class has
suffered from the direct and indirect
consequences of the Battle of London.
No improvement can be anticipated
until that trouble is over, but in the
meantime buyers and tenants may pick
up profitable bargains in sites,
houses and commercial premises.' (*Times*
Estate Market report, January 1941)

'Ministers of Morale'

(*New York Herald Tribune* describing the King and Queen)

*The King is still in London, in London, in
   London
And he would be in London Town
   if London Bridge was falling down.*
(Song lyric of 1941)

Buckingham Palace (*left*) was bombed
several times during the war. After the
first hit (on 13 September 1940) the
Queen is said to have commented, 'I'm
so glad we've been bombed. It makes
me feel I can look the East End in the
face.' The King and Queen's many
impromptu visits to blitzed areas and
their willingness to share misfortune as
they stumbled over the rubble and glass
made them greatly loved. After the war
Churchill wrote simply, 'It was a great
help to Britain to have so good a King
and Queen.'

An unexploded bomb or 'UXB'
(*above left*) was as unwelcome a visitor
in Buckingham Palace as in this terraced
cottage in south-east London.

(*Opposite below*) *Night in Dockland*, 1940
by Feliks Topolski.

'Mummy, I can't go to sleep yet .

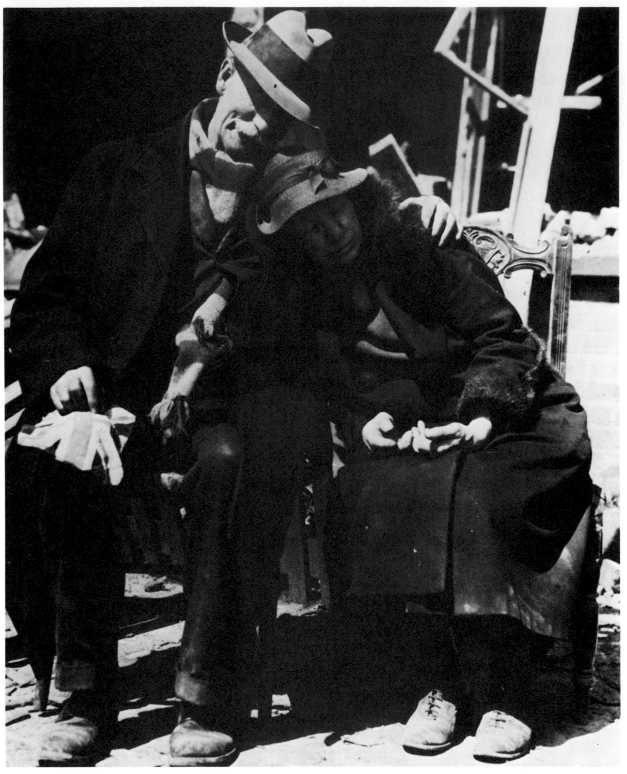

'Now here it must be very definitely stated that the objectives in London at which our Air Force aim are all of either military nature or of those industrial categories pertaining to England's war effort.' (Hamburg Broadcast, 8 September 1940)

. The siren hasn't sounded'

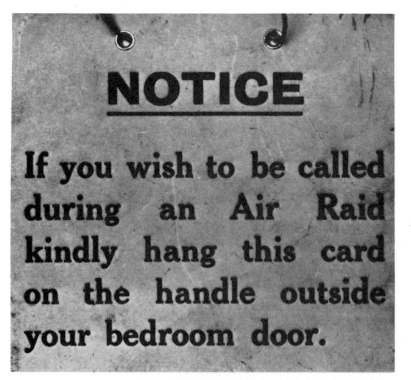

NOTICE

If you wish to be called during an Air Raid kindly hang this card on the handle outside your bedroom door.

'I take this bombing as a good sign – the last kick of a drowning man. Hitler wouldn't have done it if he hadn't been up against it.' (A tailor's manager, quoted by J. L. Hodson, 13 September 1940)

'These raids give me the feeling that Hitler appears much more worried than he seems.' (Old lady confiding to friend in a *Punch* cartoon, 11 September 1940)

They were right: Hitler had ordered the *Luftwaffe* to switch to night bombing attacks on London because of its failure to destroy British ports, aerodromes and aircraft factories in the daylight raids of the Battle of Britain.

'Are you down-hearted?' . . . 'No!'

(Churchill's familiar question and answer)

The bomb in Mrs Miniver's drawing room (*above*) was as unshocking and well-bred as Mrs Miniver herself . . . and quite unlike the real thing.

Narrator: 'What's the Three Lamps like now?'
Customer: 'It isn't like anything. It isn't there. It's nothing mun. You remember Ben Evans's stores? It's right next door to that. Ben Evans isn't there either.'
(From *Return Journey* [to Swansea], BBC script by Dylan Thomas)

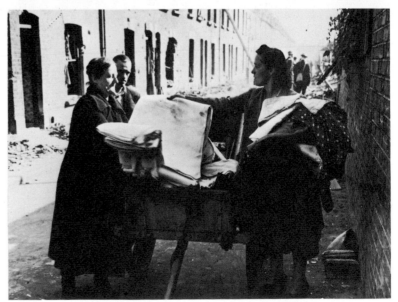

. . . sometimes the answer was 'Yes!'

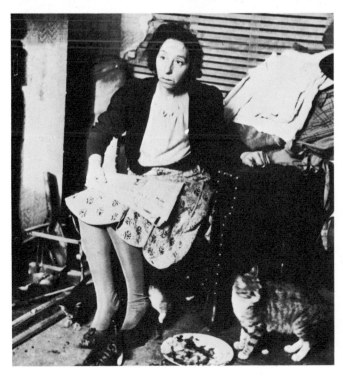

'London is facing riots, the authorities prove to be helpless, and everywhere there is wildest confusion.'
(German broadcast to Germany, 3 October 1940)

an unconquerable people . . .' (Churchill)

" *I think we've just got time for a Hot Bovril, old man.*"

Hot Bovril cheers!

'I see the damage done by the enemy attacks; but I also see, side by side with the devastation and amid the ruins, quiet, confident, bright and smiling eyes, beaming with a consciousness of being associated with a cause far higher and wider than any human or personal issue. I can see the spirit of an unconquerable people.' (Winston Churchill, 12 April 1941)

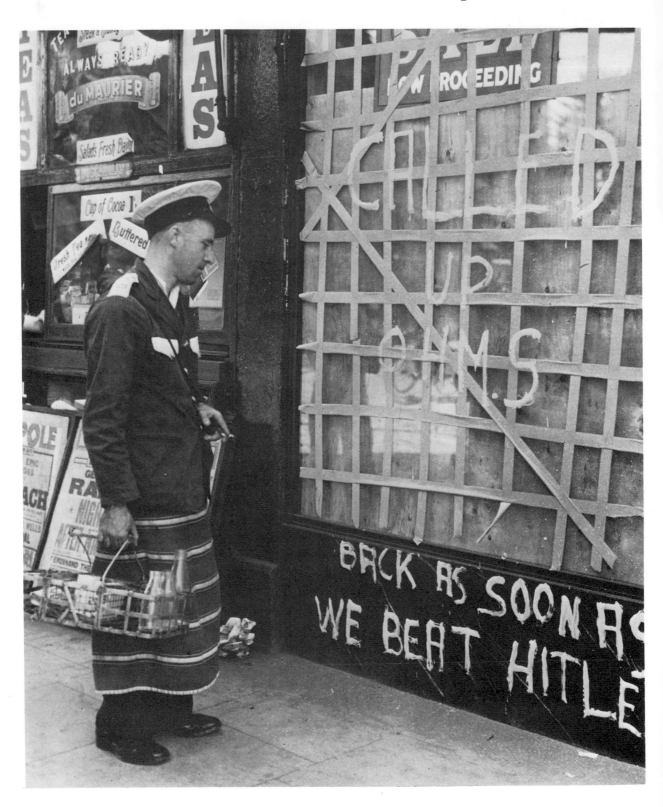

WE CAN TAKE IT

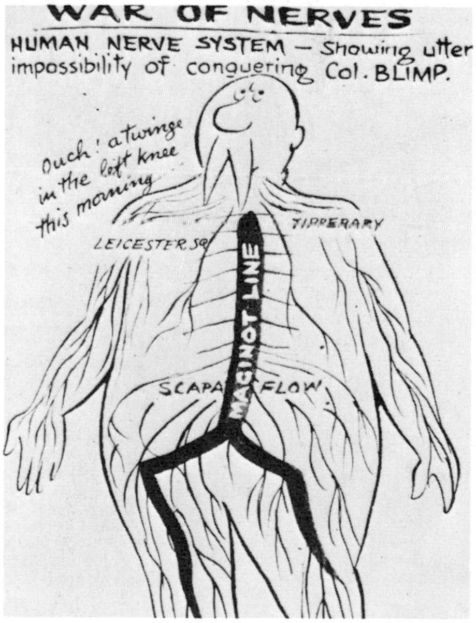
WAR OF NERVES
HUMAN NERVE SYSTEM – Showing utter impossibility of conquering Col. BLIMP.
Ouch! a twinge in the left knee this morning
LEICESTER SQ
TIPPERARY
MAGINOT LINE
SCAPA FLOW

LONDON LULLABY

1. I am a draughtsman in a "hush-hush" department. One night, after working late, I got back to my digs to find I wasn't allowed in—time bomb near. Dead tired, I dragged myself through the black-out to my cousin Jack's.

2. Jack's family were in their cellar shelter. He kept turning on the light. His wife Mary made endless cups of tea. And the children were restless. I slept through most of it, but didn't get much good out of my sleep.

3. I felt fit for nothing in the morning and it took me over an hour to get to the office, standing the whole way, first in the long queue at the bus-stop and then in the bus itself. I wasn't so fresh when I arrived.

4. I couldn't get on with my work as well as I should. I didn't blame the chief when he said I wasn't exactly helping to win the war. "What," I asked myself, "shall I be like after months of this?"

5. Johnson, at the next drawing-board, always merry and bright, gave me a tip. "What you want, old boy," he said, "is 1st Group Sleep. There are 3 Sleep Groups, and 1st Group Sleep is the kind we all need. You want to take Horlicks."

6. I took his advice. That night at Jack's we all had hot Horlicks, and we had it every night after that. The kids couldn't get enough of it and we all felt the good it was doing us. I wasn't even wakened by Jack's snoring!

7. I am a new man now. I am fitter than I have been for a long time. I don't mind the journey to the office and the chief says that if there were more like me — well, Hitler would throw in the towel!

THERE ARE THREE SLEEP GROUPS

SCIENTISTS divide us into 1st, 2nd and 3rd Group Sleepers. The last group are wakeful, can't get to sleep. Group No. 2 may sleep 8 or 9 hours, yet wake still feeling tired. Only Group 1 sleepers get the deep, refreshing, restorative sleep we need to-day.

A cup of hot Horlicks last thing at night will give you 1st Group Sleep. It will help you to take the second year of the war in your stride. Prices from 2/-; the same as before the war. At all chemists and grocers.

HORLICKS

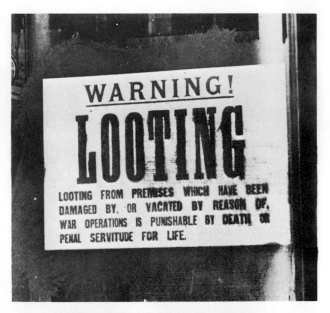

WARNING!
LOOTING
LOOTING FROM PREMISES WHICH HAVE BEEN DAMAGED BY, OR VACATED BY REASON OF, WAR OPERATIONS IS PUNISHABLE BY DEATH OR PENAL SERVITUDE FOR LIFE.

TEA ROOM.

WILLS' GOLD FLAKE CIGARETTES

. as usual

Wisecracks among the ruins –
shopkeepers' signs (1940–1):
'We've had a close shave. Come and get
one yourself.'
'Blast!'
'Gone with the Wind.'
'I have no pane dear mother now.'
'More open than usual.'
'If your knees knock kneel on them.'
(Outside a church)

'Bombed? Yes! But you should see what
the RAF has done to our branch in
Berlin!' (Outside a factory on the
Kingston by-pass)
'Be good. We are still open.' (Outside a
police station)

'We are wide open'

(Sign outside a shop, October 1940)

'Take a letter . . .'

'All England Listens'

(Priestley's own title for his *Collected Postscripts*)

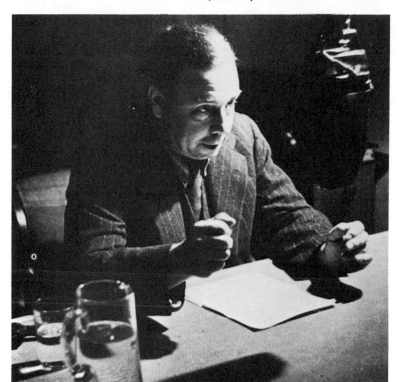

A: Ah bet tha heard Churchill.
B: Aye – I did.
A: He doesn't half give it to them. I carn't go to sleep when he's on. He's the best talker we have. (Conversation in Bolton, October 1939)

(*Below*) Listening to Churchill, August 1941, and (*left*) J. B. Priestley on the air.

In 1940 Churchill had a broadcasting rival, J. B. Priestley, whose *Postcripts* after the Sunday evening news were originally begun as an answer to Lord Haw-Haw. 'What is it that is giving Mr Priestley a radio following in this country which must be almost as big as Mr Churchill's?' asked the *Yorkshire Post* in July 1940, answering itself that, 'It is the sound of his voice that England finds so welcome and reassuring.' His message was more welcome and reassuring still. He described things not only as they were but as they might be. To Churchill, who believed 'the one aim is victory', Priestley seemed dangerously left-wing in wanting not just victory, but a just society.

'This is a war of the unknown warriors'

(Churchill, 1940)

To the ARP and the AFS a fire, however spectacular, was just 'an incident'. Before the Blitz the ARP warden was looked on with anything from cool indifference to mild amusement; from envy (as a paid army-dodger) to suspicion (as a Peeping Tom peering through cracks in blackout curtains). All this changed in 1940:

> 'But 'e's Saviour of 'is country
> When the guns begin to shoot.'

In February 1941 at the height of the Blitz an ordinary fireman (even if he was a poet like Stephen Spender), in the London fire brigade got £3 12s a week plus 10s rent money, an AFS £3 5s plus a meals allowance. He played down the heroics as much as any Battle of Britain pilot. 'There's nothing really exciting about being on top of a turn-table ladder – you get used to it, like most other things.' But a *Picture Post* photographer who went into action with the London Firemen during the Blitz expressed the strain: 'When it's all over . . . watch them grey-eyed and haggard trying to dry their drenched clothes and nearly dropping with exhaustion while the station radio plays "Keep your thumbs up and say it's Tiggerty Boo".'

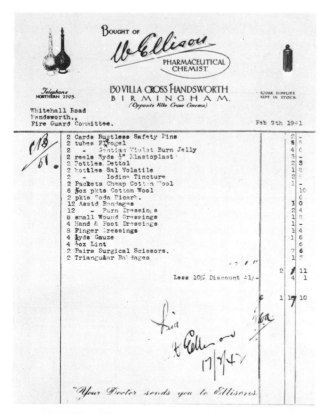

2	Cards Rustless Safety Pins	2	
2	tubes Flavogel	5	5
2	- Gentian Violet Burn Jelly	4	6
2	reels 3yds ½" Elastoplast	3	-
2	Bottles. Dettol	2	3
1	bottles Sal Volatile	1	6
2	Iodine Tincture	2	5
2	Packets Cheap Cotton Wool	1	-
6	½oz pkts Cotton Wool		10
2	pkts Soda Bicarb.		6
12	Asstd Bandages	1	0
12	- Burn Dressings	2	4
8	small Wound Dressings	1	8
4	Hand & Foot Dressings	1	-
8	Finger Dressings	1	4
4	½yds Gauze	1	6
4	½oz Lint		6
2	Pairs Surgical Scissors.	7	6
2	Triangular Bandages	1	5

Less 10% Discount 41/-

HOW TO TACKLE FIRE BOMBS

When fire bombs fall indoors or where they can start a fire they should be tackled resolutely and at once. As some will contain high explosive, always take best available cover. Leave all fire bombs alone—if they fall where they can do no particular harm.

'The warden's day came, and it was a glorious one,' *Front Line*, the Ministry of Home Security's own wartime story of Civil Defence explained. 'He (or she) was the eyes and ears of the Control Centre in the field; and the chartered "good neighbour" of the Blitz.' The good warden, whilst 'not afraid to be gentle and kind,' knew how to tackle a fire bomb (*above*), how to equip his post with first aid supplies (*above left* a Birmingham chemist's invoice of goods supplied in February 1941 to the Handsworth Fire Guard Committee), and 'how to find and succour the injured' (*opposite above right*). The heavy rescue man became 'the new technician of the Blitz', specializing in 'the behaviour of broken buildings'.

(*Left*) A fireman, still in pyjamas, rests by the ruins of Exeter after a 'Baedeker raid' (shown also in William Clause's painting *opposite below*). (*Opposite above right*) Drawing by Clifford Hall, 1941.

We shall fight in the offices .

THE INCENDIARY BOMB MENACE: FIRE FIGHTING IN OFFICE BUILDINGS.

Drawn by our Special Artist G. H. Davis, with the Assistance of the Fire Protection Services of the City of Westminster.

. and in the hospitals

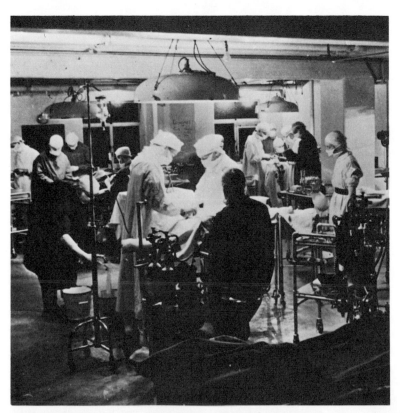

The operating theatre at Guy's Hospital (*left*) carried on in the basement. It was equipped with four tables, typically all in use during a busy night in the Blitz. One doctor wrote of 'the hectic times when it often seemed that the whole of the elaborately-arranged casualty services of the London region must break down'. Yet London had been prepared for even more casualties (after exaggerated prophecies based on Spanish Civil War experience) and at the outbreak of war Herbert Morrison had requisitioned vast numbers of papier mâché coffins – never to be used.

A wide range of emergency social services for the bombed-out was set up in an equally wide range of buildings such as this converted and requisitioned dance-hall (*below*). Some of the special hostels, social clubs and welfare centres set up to cope with the emergency became permanent. Warfare meant welfare.

History, not Grammar

DON'T FENCE ME IN

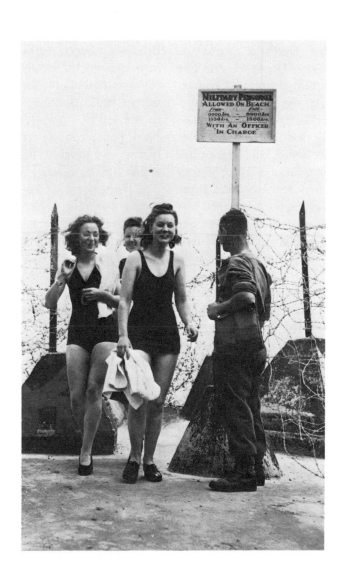

*Oh, give me land, lots of land under starry skies
    above,
Don't fence me in.
Let me ride through the wide open country that
    I love,
Don't fence me in.*

Whether you lived in a great city which had been
blitzed or in a small village which seldom even saw
or heard a German aeroplane in the starry skies
above, England seemed a very small place during
most of the war. Indeed, those Englishmen and
women who were quarantined in their own
country, were prepared to sing as lustily as any
Texan 'Don't Fence Me In', one of the favourite
popular songs of 1944 when the first quarantine
had just been lifted on D-Day. The fencing-in had
been psychological and administrative, of course,
as much as geographical. It was not only movements in and out of the country which had been
controlled. 'Living in London', wrote Charles
Ritchie, the Canadian diplomat, in September
1939, 'is like being an inmate of a reformatory
school. Everywhere you turn you run into some
regulation designed for your own protection. The
Government is like the School Matron with her
keys jangling at her waist. She orders you about,
good humouredly enough, but all the same in no
uncertain terms.'

Even before the 'real war' began and the Allies
and the GIs arrived, the restrictions had multiplied
. . . along with the blue pencils. Indeed whatever
else may have been phoney about the phoney war,
the restrictions were not. And one place where
people had never objected to being fenced in –
before their 'ain firesides' – was no longer secure
when the Englishman's (and the Welshman's and
the Scotsman's) home could become a billet instead
of a castle. The first invasion of the war was the
arrival of the evacuees, and many people thought
evacuation should have been made compulsory for
the evacuees as it was for their hosts.

The enabling measure which gave the government powers over every aspect of Englishmen's
lives was the Emergency Powers (Defence) Bill,
which became law on 24 August 1939. 'One day,'
as E. S. Turner put it with some exaggeration,
'sufficed to turn Britain into a totalitarian state.'
Many restrictions were the result of the blackout:
on Guy Fawkes' Day 1939, children had to go
without fireworks, and on Christmas Eve worship-
pers had to go without midnight services because
of the difficulty of blacking-out large stained glass
windows. There was also a general prohibition on
the operation of any siren, hooter, whistle, rattle,
bell, horn, gong or similar instrument, except in
accordance with official instructions, which affected
everyone from muffin men and carol singers to
munitions workers and the Forces themselves.

One reaction to the 'laws against it' was laughter,
Britain's 'secret weapon'. In September 1939 Sir
Seymour Hicks, newly-appointed head of ENSA
(Entertainments National Service Association), said
on the radio that laughter was an important asset
in the job of winning the war and one which the
Nazis conspicuously lacked. Fortunately the British
had it, and much irritation about the new regulations was harmlessly defused in jokes, although
The Times portentously condemned 'the danger of
jocose optimism which refuses to face unpleasant
facts to which, as a people, we have shown a
tendency'. A whole new world of jokes about
evacuees, the blackout, rationing and the ARP
appeared, and the warden quickly replaced the
window-cleaner in peeping-Tom-style folk lore.

As self-appointed Minister of Aggravation and
Mysteries, a real Tom, ITMA's ('It's That Man
Again') Tommy Handley, caught the phoney war
mood of frustration with (although never rebellion
against) petty rules and restrictions. In his ITMA
broadcast of 12 December 1939 he announced, 'It
is my duty tonight on the umpteenth day of the
war against Depression to explain to you that I
have seven hundred further restrictions to impose
upon you . . . some of the most irritating regulations you've ever heard of.' The new rules included
'coupons for kisses', 'the prohibition of bath water
(later to come almost true with the 5 inch bath of
1942) and Tommy's own 'wife-restriction'.

The first official censors are said to have laughed

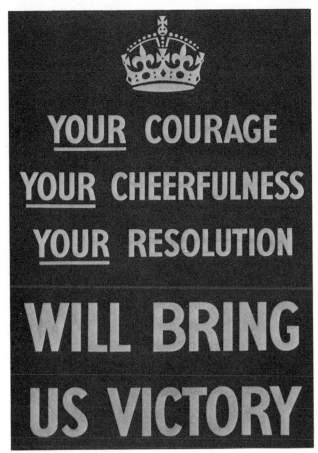

YOUR COURAGE
YOUR CHEERFULNESS
YOUR RESOLUTION
WILL BRING
US VICTORY

These broadcasts encouraged a kind of rumour-spreading that even a successful Ministry of Information would have been powerless to prevent. As it was, the Ministry did its best to dissuade the public from listening to them even during the phoney war when they were as effective an antidote to 'boredom and dullness' as television might have been. Later, when the war hotted up, it was legitimate for *Everybody* to ask, 'Would you ask a traitor into your house night after night?', if unwise of it to go on (in vain) to demand jamming of

Kidnapping Lord Haw-Haw

when they discovered that their blue pencils were all stamped 'Made in Bavaria'. But there is little evidence of belly laughter (though there may have been giggles) in London University's Senate House where the real Ministry of Information's officials were housed. They may have taken as an early motto 'Give us the straw and we will drop the bricks', but, not surprisingly, given their background, they tended to be out of touch with 'common people'. They were described in a letter to America by F. Tennyson Jesse as 'Ex-civil servants, ornithologists, left-wing pamphleteers, professors . . . who have busied themselves in either warning us of dangers which do not exist or issuing consolatory "pap" to people who are in no need of anything but to be told the truth.' The patronizing tone struck by some of the posters drew as sharp a contrast between 'them' and 'us' as Lord Haw-Haw himself was trying to do in his broadcasts.

German radio. 'German lies over the air', said the Ministry, 'are like parachute troops dropping on Britain – they are all part of the plan to get us down . . . switch 'em off or tune 'em out!'

The number of listeners to Lord Haw-Haw diminished after Dunkirk, though during the invasion scare reports of his uncanny local knowledge (investigated by a special Ministry of Information sub-committee) attracted new listeners, particularly when bombs had fallen or it was feared that they were about to fall. Mass Observation collected enough information to show that what listeners said Lord Haw-Haw had said was at least as unreliable as what he had actually said. But then the war, after all, blurred many impressions. Churchill himself, when he read the *Daily Mirror* (which he thought was almost as anxious as Lord Haw-Haw to stir up 'class and party dissensions') did not always understand what it said, and when Herbert Morrison saw a Zec cartoon on 6 March 1942 he did not understand what it meant; he moved, with the support of Churchill and Ernest Bevin, to suppress the paper.

The kind of cartoons which *were* approved of in official circles incorporated 'joke Germans' who, it was felt, were always good for a healthy laugh, and they appeared not only in cartoons but in comics, songs ('Der Führer's Face') and commercial films. In *The Goose Steps Out* Will Hay infiltrates a Nazi spy school and prepares the pupils to meet the English.

'"Now Klaus," someone says to you, "well, what do you think of the news, mate?" What would you reply?'

'I should say, "By Jove, old fruit, I find it increasingly disheartening. I fear we Britons are no match for the Glorious German Army" . . .' For the colonel in ITMA a 'sly Jerry' naturally came across as a 'dry sherry' ('I don't mind if I do'), whilst Nat Gubbins, not 'fenced in' but *Sitting on the Fence*, forgot our own shelters and imagined a shelter conversation somewhere in Germany:

'Vot vos dot?'

'Dot vos a bompf.'

'All der time dere iss bompfs.'

'Ven vill der war over be?'

'For dot question asking Hermann to der concentration camp yesterday vos sent. Heil, Hitler.'

'Heil, Hitler.'

'To-night ve vill again der liddle joke make und der merry games play. Dere vos a very fonny joke vich ask vy in der desert a man does not hongry go.'

'Vell, vy in der desert a man does not hungry go?'

'A man in der desert does not hongry go because

of der sand vich in der desert iss.'

'Poddon?'

'I repeat dot a man in der desert does not hongry go because of der sand vich in der desert iss. Der sandvich in der desert iss.'

'Dot very fonny vos. Heil, Hitler.'

'Heil, Hitler.' . . .

'Der newspaper Diplomatische und Politische Damrubbische say dot by to-morrow der Jugo-Slavs in der Greater Reich vill be.'

'Der Diplomatische Damrubbische und Politische mit Gibberische und Sauerkraut say dot by der next day der Turks in der Greater Reich vill be.'

'Der Diplomatischedamgibberische und Politischedamrubbische mit Sauerkraut und Saussische Stuffed mit Garbische say dot by der day after all der Balkans in der Greater Reich vill be. Heil, Hitler.'

'Heil, Hitler.'

'Vot vos dot?'

'Dot vos a bompf.'

'Und dot und dot?'

'Dot vos more bompfs.'

'All der time dere iss bompfs.'

Even in the most threatening days of expected invasion in summer 1940 people made jokes about German parachutists, often, as the rumour had it, dressed as nuns, invariably displaying their hairy legs and carrying the regulation *sauerkraut* and German sausages. Later still, a London cinema audience roared with laughter when a newsreel commentator, reporting the arrival of Hess in May 1941, said that even the arrival of Goering wouldn't cause surprise, adding in his fruity Movietone voice, 'I hope he brings his ration card.'

In May 1940, as the greatest battle in history was being fought across the Channel, the fences were built even higher as the British people were given what one American observer described as 'the stiffest dose of totalitarian principles that a democracy has ever had to swallow in order to save the democratic ideal from total extinction'. When Churchill introduced a new piece of legislation which required all persons 'to place them-

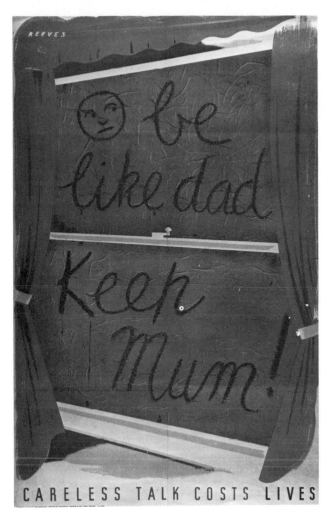

CARELESS TALK COSTS LIVES

a child to say, untruthfully, 'I don't know'.) As spy fever grew more intense during the invasion scare, a rash of road blocks and observation posts rapidly spread over a countryside devoid of sign-posts and other identifying names. At the same time and for the same reason, while places lost their identity BBC announcers found their own. They gave their names, most of which became household words (in the familiar phrase 'and this is [e.g.] Bruce Belfrage reading it'), to make it more difficult for the enemy successfully to impersonate them. The swing pianist Charlie Kunz was the victim of hysterical accusations that he was transmitting messages to the enemy by a code concealed in the notes he played. The ringing of church bells was banned for the duration except as a warning of invasion by parachutists and it was the surest sign of 'the end of the beginning' when they were allowed to ring out again on 15 November 1942 to celebrate Monty's victory in North Africa.

The Ministry of Information was in charge of anti-'careless talk' propaganda, both in 1940 and on the eve of D-Day in 1944, which even put fences around people's conversation. It was designed to check the spreading of rumours and of 'alarm and despondency' as well as actual information about troop-movements and convoy sailings. Mistakenly in 1940 the Ministry even tried (though unsuccessfully) to convince people that the best defence against the Fifth Column was the 'Silent Column'. 'Keep Out – This is a Private War,' was *Picture Post*'s rejoinder. 'The War Office, the Admiralty and the Air Ministry and the Ministry of Information are engaged in a war against the Nazis. They are on no account to be disturbed. Nothing is to be photographed. No one is to come near. By Order.' Churchill himself eventually killed off the Silent Column idea. Yet the sense of a hush-hush private war persisted. The words of a song sung to the tune of 'My Bonny lies over the Ocean' ran:

My Bonny is stationed at — —
It's just as hush hush as can be
So nobody knows he's at — —
Except all his relations and me.
The gun he is guarding at — —

selves, their services and their property at the disposal of His Majesty' a coster-monger on a donkey cart expressed the general emotional relief that at last a fighting leader was ready to take drastic action against the enemy: 'That's right! All in it together to knock 'is bleedin' block off!' Mr Attlee expressed the same view in more dignified language: 'There must be no laggards. Victory is our goal. We must and shall attain it.'

People accepted – even welcomed – a huge package of new restrictions designed to tell them 'what to do if the enemy comes'. It was forbidden for example, to tell a stranger the way, and even children were taught, 'If anyone stops me to ask the way, all I must answer is "I can't say".' (This formula neatly avoided the moral issue of teaching

Stretches seventy feet in the air
And though you mayn't say you have seen it,
You — — well know that it's there.

A few places with persisting names were surrounded by all-too-real fences – the Channel Islands, for example, where German and British signposts were curiously juxtaposed along with German and British people. The islands were turned into 'forts' by 1943 after thousands of greenhouses had been blown up near their coasts. *Deutsche Guernsey Zeitung* was writing in July 1942 not of English humour but of 'Englische Nervosität'.

In another off-shore island, the Isle of Man, there had been a different mix of British and very different Germans in 1940. At the outbreak of war about two thousand suspect 'enemy aliens' had been rounded up and interned and another 6,800, whose 'reliability was uncertain', were placed in Category B. Yet they were all well-treated, and one of the first propaganda films of the war, *The First Days*, a sensible, tolerant documentary when it showed aliens registering on the outbreak of war, added the mild comment that 'they are part of London, part of her social culture'. By May 1940, however, moods had changed and the *Daily Mail* was not alone in urging 'intern the lot'.

During the summer of 1940 thousands of them were impounded in the Isle of Man, with 'no hope of consolation'. 'The British Government', explained the *New Statesman* on 3 August, 'reckons as suspect anyone who does not carry a British passport.' The internees included writers, artists, scientists and scholars, many of them victims of Hitler, who had fled to democratic Britain. An MP called this, at the time, 'a bespattered page of our history', but a more memorable comment comes in the last sentence of a WVS report written by Mrs Montagu Norman who had accompanied a group of 'female aliens' from London to Liverpool. 'After a good lunch at the Adelphi WVS felt better, but at night I was haunted by the thought of those unfortunate women sitting in that grim old stadium, mere victims of Hitler's crime.'

For most English people real 'fencing in' seemed an appropriate way of handling not only aliens but all fascists, Nazis and the like, and there was a public outcry when in November 1943 a sick Sir Oswald Mosley was released on the orders of Morrison. Nine people out of ten felt that he should not be released. They were also prepared to be 'fenced in' by rules and regulations themselves if they thought they were necessary, although this did not mean that there were no conscientious objectors (even to fire-watching) or that voluntary effort was not prized as much as government orders.

A new kind of 'fencing in' started with the Blitz, when fire-watchers were in the greatest demand – not just fencing in through rules and regulations but internment down in the shelters . . . shelters against bombs that respected persons even less than bureaucrats did. J. L. Hodson graphically described the scene in Piccadilly underground station in October 1940:

If you can imagine a seaside resort on Bank Holiday, promenade and steps and sands littered with people sleeping out in grotesque attitudes, surrounded by suitcases and thermos flasks, with young children and babies worn out and sleeping, and transfer that picture to tube platforms, odd corners and staircases, you get a mild idea of what it is like. People sleep where you would have thought sleep was impossible to achieve. On the other hand many bring eiderdowns, blankets, pillows and turn platforms into beds.

The Government had never intended the Tubes to be used permanently as shelters, fearing squalor and disease less than some mysterious 'deep shelter mentality'. It wished, too, to keep every line of transport clear for troop movements. However, there was nothing illegal in your buying a platform ticket for 1½d and not travelling . . . The Government's long-promised deep shelters – four north of the Thames and four south – were ready only in time for the 'little blitz' of early 1944.

There were some very strange features of the new 'fenced in' existence. The Government was willing in time to provide toilets – and these were doubtless welcomed – but the bunks it also provided were not always welcomed, on the grounds that fewer people could crowd into a given area

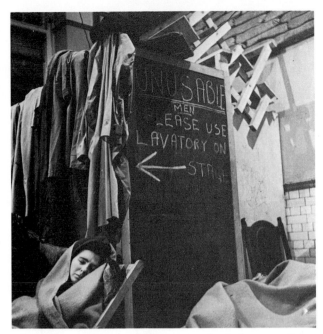

suits 'easily zipped and ready to go' (one Butterick pattern for a 'siren suit' even suggested optimistically, 'should peace come sooner than anticipated, it can be turned into a playsuit'.) There were songbooks for the dug-out; knitting patterns for Balaclava helmets 'to keep shelter draughts off the head'. The Government itself gave advice on how to keep warm and comfortable in the Anderson with a home-made heater 'made with two large flower pots and a candle', whilst one women's magazine suggested taking a hot sandbag to the shelter to guard against cold feet.

As the shelters emptied in the summer of 1941 and in 1942 other kinds of controls increased. Indeed, people got more and more, not less and less, fenced in as the war went on, with a whole batch of new manpower regulations in December 1941 (including the end of 'block reservations' and, for the first time, the conscription of women) and of Crippsian austerity controls on the economy in February 1942, controls which went further than Churchill's had done in 1940 and which outlasted Cripps. They were welcomed ... significantly at the very time that Army 'bull-shit' was most under attack. 'The great silent, courageous mass of people who make up Britain's real strength will gladly pull in their belts until it hurts,' Mollie Panter-Downes reported back to New York in July 1942 when shortages of every variety were acute. And even pulling in belts was not all. 'Tell us to cut our throats for goodness sake and we'll do it,' was how one observer summed up popular attitudes, 'but not until you tell us to.'

It was in such a mood that the British people not only got used to controls (as they had got used to sustained voluntary effort) but argued for their extension in controls that would ensure 'fair shares for all'; citizenship controls; controls that would involve nationalization of private property, socialist controls; controls that Beaverbrook and Churchill, who had imposed so many of them, tried in vain to persuade the people to remove in 1945. The first fire after the war was not however, to be the bonfire of controls. That came later, years after the war was over.

of platform. The stench was so bad that sensitive souls preferred to brave existence overground, but many people do not seem to have minded too much. A police sergeant at King's Cross said he thought there were six thousand people in the underground there. 'They seem pretty happy' was his cautious verdict.

Some accounts of the war give the impression that most Londoners spent their nights in the tube, but a shelter census taken in November 1940 showed that in Central London only four per cent of the population was sleeping in the Underground, compared with nine per cent in public shelters and twenty-seven per cent in domestic shelters, which usually meant an Anderson in the garden. (The Morrison shelter, which 'looked like a dining-table and can be used as one' ... 'was made of steel strong enough to stand up under almost anything except a direct hit with high explosives', but it was not introduced until March 1941, towards the end of the worst months of the Blitz.)

Shelter life created a whole new sub-culture which inspired its own artists, such as Henry Moore and Edward Ardizzone; its own amusements and games; and its own fashion consisting of shelter

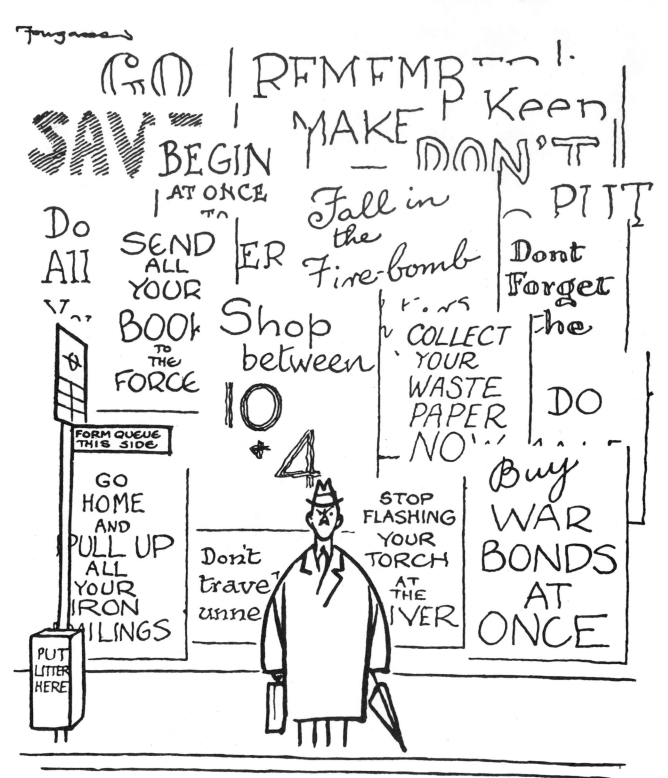

"If only they'd tell us all what to do."

. there's a war on?

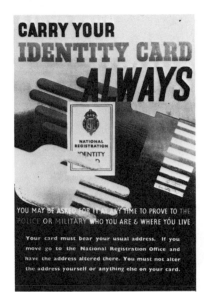

In November 1939 Mass Observation's national panel of part-time observers collected the main grumbles from all over England. Giving the largest, blackout, as index — 100, the results were as follows:

Main grumbles	Town	Country
Blackout	100	100
Food	66	68
Fuel, petrol	44	50
Evacuation	37	64
Prices	42	39
Lack of amusements	30	21
Transport	38	14
Lack of news	36	21

(*New Statesman*, 13 January 1940)

Red tape might have been added to the list of grumbles in 1941. (*Left*) A farmer struggles with his paperwork; (*below*) an identity check.

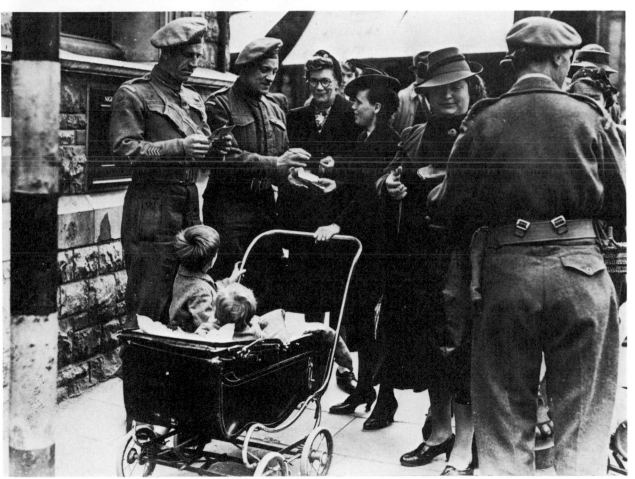

'Banned for the duration'.

" *Aha—sketching the weather, eh?!!!* "

. or just blacked out

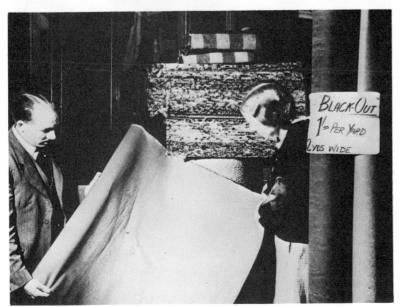

A blackout warden passin' yelled,
  'Ma, pull down that blind;
Just look at what you're showin', and we
  Shouted, 'Never Mind.' Ooh!
Knees Up, Mother Brown! Knees Up,
  Mother Brown . . .
(1939 version of First World War song)

'One defendant, fined £2, asserted he did
not know he had to blackout the back of
his house as well as the front.' (*Birmingham
Post*, 16 September 1939)

Big houses posed big (blackout)
problems. (*Above left*) The butler lends
a hand.

'Intern the lot'

The Channel Islands were the only British territories to be occupied and ruled by the Nazis. The islanders felt isolated and abandoned – under curfew – as indeed they were, the British Government having decided not to defend them in June 1940. The occupation, with full German trappings, lasted until the end of the war, the military leaders of the second front being unwilling in 1944 to divert energy from the main campaign sweeping across France. It was not until VE-Day that Churchill gave the news that 'Our dear Channel Islands are also to be freed today.'

The Isle of Man with its internment camp at Douglas was as much a prison as the Channel Islands but in this case the British were the jailers. Fred Uhlman, an anti-Nazi Jewish barrister, now dubbed a Class B enemy alien, was among them (despite having an English wife). After a few weeks at Ascot in Bertram Mills' Circus winter quarters (used as a transit camp) (*above right*), he was sent to Douglas: 'Imagine a square in the middle of London consisting of some forty small and cheap lodging houses. Surround it with barbed wire, and fill each house with between thirty and forty men of all ages and professions. Imagine all windows painted blue and all electric light bulbs red (giving us by day the light of an aquarium, at night that – even more incongruous – of a brothel); and you have some notion of the Hutchinson Square Camp at Douglas.'

Luckily when arrested he had in his pocket a small bottle of indian ink, a stick of charcoal and a pen. The drawing (*above right*) was one of many he did in captivity.

'Our dear Channel Islands . . .'

'Tittle-tattle lost the battle'

(Government anti-'careless talk' slogan, 1940)

Careless talk – Canadian style. (Canadian Government poster, 1940)

Four posters by Fougasse

(*Above*) *Off to the Shelter* by Edward Ardizzone.

(*Below*) *Sleeping in the Shelter* by Edward Ardizzone.

'Against infection and the hand of war'

(Shakespeare, *Richard II*)

SHARE THE SHELTER

but don't share the germs!

Britain has been faced with the grave problem of "Shelter-infection". Dozens, scores, hundreds, sometimes thousands of people are herded together for long nights in a confined space — sharing each others' breath, sneezes, coughs, germs.

"What can prevent epidemics arising?" asked doctors, Medical Officers of Health, Government officials.

Lord Horder's Committee found the answer in two words — *sodium hypochlorite*. The hypochlorite principle of disinfection has long been known to bacteriologists. Its value was recognised by scientists in the *last* war. In last year's Lister Memorial Lecture before the Royal College of Surgeons it was cited as "the ideal antiseptic", because of its cleansing and germ-killing powers.

But it was not until the advent of Milton that a stable, harmless, *practical* form of hypochlorite was evolved. Milton brought hypochlorite into our homes and everyday lives. Now, after ten years of research, the Milton laboratories have made possible the *sterilisation of air* with Hypochlorite.

The results are astonishing. Eminent bacteriologists testify that by spraying Milton into the atmosphere, air-borne germs can be reduced "by as much as 94%". The spray deodorises the air, too — immediately, almost unbelievably.

Thus a big problem has found a solution. Is *your* refuge or shelter "Miltonised?" Milton costs 8d., 1/4, 1/11 and 3/4 a bottle (including Purchase Tax) from all Chemists.

What the authorities are doing:
Many Local Authorities are already using Milton either in hand sprays or the electric Drysaliver. Special arrangements have been made for such authorities to obtain Milton in bulk at advantageous terms. Application should be made to Milton Proprietary Ltd., John Milton House, London, N. 5, who will gladly supply full information.

What you can do:
If you sleep at home in a refuge room or private shelter you can use your ordinary Milton nasal spray. Put three teaspoonsful of Milton into the spray container and fill with water up to the neck. A few squirts on the spray bulb, and the air needed you is clean, fresh and sterilised. The Milton Nasal Spray costs 3/6 from any Chemist.

Order (*above left and right*) . . . and chaos (*below left*) in the shelters.

'When you get over the shock of seeing so many sprawling people, you are overcome with the smell of humanity and dirt. Dirt abounds everywhere. The floors are never swept and are filthy. People are sleeping on piles of rubbish. The passages are loaded with dirt. There is no escaping it. The arches are dank and grim.

There they sit in darkness, head of one against feet of the next. There is no room to move, hardly any room to stretch . . .' (Description of an underground shelter by East End working girl, reported by Tom Harrisson, *New Statesman*, September 1940)

'Be a man and give a woman your place – in the shelters.' (Government slogan)

A sheltered life

As the Blitz went on, the Government, resigned to the use of Tubes as shelters, provided toilet and catering facilities. Henry Moore, spending the evenings going from shelter to shelter as an official war artist with his sketch book, commented that 'I was both excited and engaged by everything I saw around me – until it got organized and then it was no longer interesting for me.' Often, however, the 'organization' was primitive (*above*). Kingsley Martin described a vast underground food store in Stepney, 'where hundreds of poor people took shelter among crates of margarine . . . which were used as screens for unofficial lavatories'. A London woman describing her shelter experiences in the Blitz said, 'I remember being driven out because much as I was afraid of the bombs the stench was so bad that I just had to get out . . .'

(*Above*) Mrs Churchill and Herbert Morrison watch a demonstration of the new Morrison shelter in February 1941.

'The things that are going on now in these public air raid shelters are very dreadful. For a young girl to go into a public shelter now without her father and mother is simply asking for trouble.' (East London magistrate, reported in the *Evening Standard*, 4 November 1940)

They say that women, in a bombing raid
Retire to sleep in brand new underwear
Lest they be tumbled out of doors, displayed
In shabby garments to the public stare.
(Norman Cameron, *Punishment Enough*)

Like its occupants, Mrs Miniver's shelter looks too good to be true.

'Hush-hush'

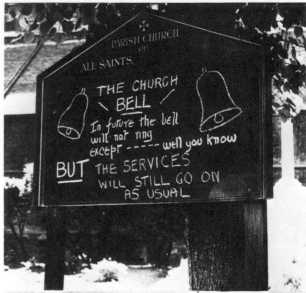

A joint Christmas card from prisoners of war in 1942 (*right*). Letters could tell more even if you had to read between the lines: 'Darling, we are treated wonderfully well here. Our billets are cosy, the food is plentiful, our guards kind. I want everybody at home to know this so tell it to your friends, tell it to the Army, tell it to the Navy, and above all, dear, tell it to the Marines.'

The ringing of church bells was banned in June 1940 (*above right*) except to warn of invasion. Apart from a false alarm in September when there was confusion over the meaning of the codeword 'Cromwell' ('conditions are ripe for invasion'), bells were next heard – at Churchill's request – to celebrate the victory of El Alamein.

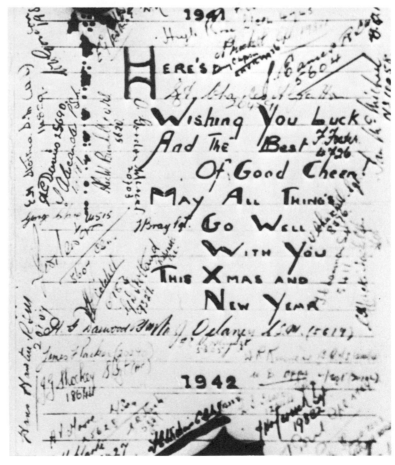

'Opened by Censor'

The Ministry of Information excelled in the traditional arts of 'cutting the spy's line of communication'. So, too, did the censors. (*Below right*) A lady censor probes a cigar for 'foreign matter'. Unfortunately, the so-called 'Mystery of Information' was equally good at cutting off the British from their own lines of communication. Even good news was nervously suppressed at the beginning of the war. The American journalist John Gunther asked one of the Ministry's censors for the text of the leaflet which the RAF dropped on Germany, only to be told, 'We are not allowed to disclose information which might be of value to the enemy.'

GUINNESS IS GOOD FOR YOU

'Knowing the form'

. . . Words speak louder than actions . . .

"May I see your driving licence, please?"

"May I see your driving licence, please, and your petrol permit and your insurance certificate and your identity cards and your authority for employment of a mechanical vehicle, and your area passes, and your registration book, and the name of your employer, and documents setting forth nature of employment and reason for which journey undertaken?"

DON'T GET AROUND MUCH ANYMORE

Missed the Saturday dance,
Heard they crowded the floor,
Couldn't bear it without you—
Don't get around much anymore.

Take your places in the queue
And say 'Toodle-loo'
We mustn't miss the last bus home.

In 1941 and 1942 the Second World War became 'global'. British soldiers, sailors and airmen might find themselves posted to any corner of the world. The war became far more of a war of movement than the First World War. Yet in 1940 everyone – including lots of foreigners – seemed to have been packed into this tiny country which would, so it was sung, always be there.

From 1940 to 1945, also, while ninety-nine out of every hundred British civilians could get out of it for neither business nor pleasure, many others, the innumerable 'Billy Browns' of London Town or elsewhere, could scarcely get around it unless they had been drafted into one of the multifarious forms of war-work. 'Mobility' for the forces, civilian war-workers and evacuees meant 'staying-put' for the rest of the community. They were related parts of the same wartime pattern.

Some of the most successful wartime propaganda posters explained why 'passenger trains have to be fewer and slower'. 'The time has come,' one of the best-known wartime posters advised portentously, 'for every person to search his conscience before making a railway journey. It is more than ever necessary to ask yourself: "Is my journey really necessary?".' The railways were a weapon of war and civilian passengers were reminded, if they needed reminding, that 'food, shells and fuel must come first'. By 1944 the number of miles covered by passenger trains had fallen to a third of the pre-war figure, but every train still in service was carrying twice as many people as in 1939. Trains transported the men and materials of the BEF to Southampton in 1939; they took the Norwegian expedition to their Scottish embarkation ports in 1940; they brought back the BEF to London from south-east ports after Dunkirk, and in 1944 they

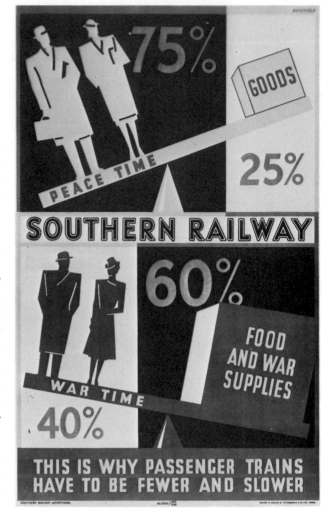

helped to assemble the great invasion army for D-Day. British Railways posters reminded the public that 'your children's food depends on the Lines behind the Lines', and that 'over half a million railwaymen are maintaining a vital national service'.

Ordinary passengers suffered from the imposition of the priorities of war, and the railways themselves suffered from every kind of shortage of manpower and materials. Despite the 'vital national service' accolade, the government had called up a hundred thousand railwaymen early in the war and, by 1943, actually had to redirect men and women to the railways.

Many railway yards had been taken over by the Ministry of Supply for making munitions. Spare parts vanished and as the war went on locomotives and carriages grew steadily older, shabbier and less efficient. Obsolete rolling stock – if it rolled at all – was kept in service until it wore out. The new Q1 'austerity class' locomotive of 1942, lacking all the traditional handsome detail of railway design, lived down to its name. By that year shortages of equipment were so desperate that the Americans sent over four hundred locomotives, some of them complete with drivers and firemen.

Travelling by train had never been so uncomfortable; nor had it ever been so expensive: fares almost tripled over the war years. The crowded corridor was as much a sign of the times as the long queues at bus stops. (Queueing there became compulsory in April 1942.) So, too, was the mood of acceptance in which most people put up with all the discomforts and waiting. During air raids trains were completely blacked out. When the siren went they had to stop at the next station to give passengers the choice of getting out of the train to take shelter or of continuing the journey at a snail's

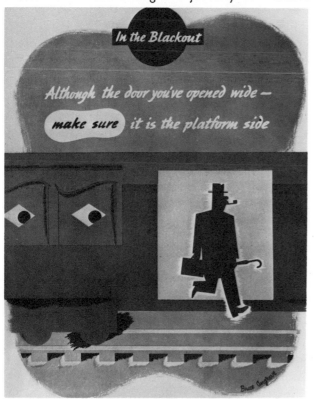

In the Blackout

Although the door you've opened wide –
make sure it is the platform side

pace (the speed limit during raids was fifteen mph until November 1940 when it was raised to twenty-five mph). As one wartime traveller put it: 'One cannot go fast enough to out-distance an aeroplane, and if they bomb the line in front of you, you couldn't pull up in time, and there you'd be in what might have been an avoidable accident.' Many passengers found the crawling pace wearing on the nerves and felt deeply, if irrationally, that they were more likely to provide a perfect target for German bombers.

Railwaymen always attracted less publicity than workers in the forces or the factories but many gave their lives to keep the trains running. Men working on 'The Lines behind the Lines' sometimes found themselves at the Front. An *Evening Standard* reporter described the courage of railwaymen during the winter of the Blitz . . .

Stations were hit and trains smashed up before they had left the platforms. Incendiaries rained down on goods yards, and railwaymen clambered over truck after truck to get at them and stifle them . . . Even while the bombs were falling, engineering parties were out, working in the dark or by the light of searchlights on some damaged portion of a line that had to be repaired. They worked all night, many times suffering casualties before the job was completed.

Buses, too, were hit by the Blitz, often literally. Others were converted into emergency ambulances and by 1941 many bus services, especially in the country, were withdrawn altogether. London lost so many buses in air raids that she had to borrow vehicles from other cities (later lending buses to Coventry and other blitzed provincial centres). Her motley collection of vehicles, many advertising strange destinations, would have confused any invading enemy.

Many bus crews displayed great courage in getting their buses through, the drivers taking strange routes in order to avoid bomb craters. In the winter of the Blitz London alone lost 156 bus- and tram-men killed and 406 injured. The same *Evening Standard* reporter described bus journeys through the darkened London streets in winter 1940.

It was eerie to sit in a bus at night with only a tiny blue light illuminating the interior, and listen to a running commentary by the girl conductress on the progress of the raid in the districts she had passed through . . . It had been bad. They did not think they would get through. Then bombs in the road had diverted them through side streets. Then there was that awful crossing over the river where they felt they were a sitting pheasant for all the bombs out of the sky. Now here they were in Fleet Street lumbering on towards Pimlico, while the heavens were alight with gun flashes and flare . . . These were the real citizens of London, who kept the capital going when the drones had gone.

Often, the drones had gone to the races. Crowded car parks at race meetings were the cause of much public resentment (and, incidentally, the source of a famous line from the popular film about the dangerous Atlantic crossing of a tanker, *San Demetrio, London*: 'That ought to be enough to take quite a few race-goers to Newmarket.'). On the whole, however, the empty car park was one more sign of the times . . . especially after the basic petrol ration was abolished in July 1942.

From the outbreak of war the private motorist had not been left only to the promptings of his conscience. Petrol rationing had begun on 16 September 1939, when branded petrol was replaced by 'pool', a medium octane blend, and petrol for commercial vehicles was dyed red to prevent its illicit use by civilians. In fact there was a good deal of petrol fiddling, some of which involved straining red petrol through a gas mask filter to get rid of the colour. Other motorists simply bought petrol on the black market. It was said to cost about 6s 6d a gallon (compared with the legal price of 'pool' which was 1s 6d in September 1939), and most car owners knew of some co-operative garage who could produce a tankful.

When petrol rationing had started, every motorist was entitled to a basic monthly ration of petrol, the quantity varying with the horsepower of the car, from four gallons for a baby Austin (price in 1939 £108) to ten gallons for cars of 20 hp and over. The most expensive new model in a 1939 catalogue, a £279 12 hp Singer drophead

coupé, said to 'combine lively acceleration with perfect safety', would have entitled its owner to seven gallons. By 1940 Ford, 'ever marching on', was advertising the Anglia, 'a car produced for wartime – and a car which would make its mark in easy days of peace! . . . It is built to give exceptional mileage on "pool" petrol . . . It meets what everybody needs these days.'

Certainly all motorists thought they needed more petrol. 'Supplementary' petrol coupons could be claimed for extra domestic or business needs or (after October 1940) for the government's 'Help Your Neighbour' free lifts scheme. Motorists who

Truck Drivers Help London Workers Reach Their Offices on Time

displayed a special sticker inside their windscreens could use their cars with a clear conscience, knowing that they were co-operating with the official view that 'a vacant place in a car travelling to or from Central London calls for an explanation'. Hitch-hiking had become government sponsored.

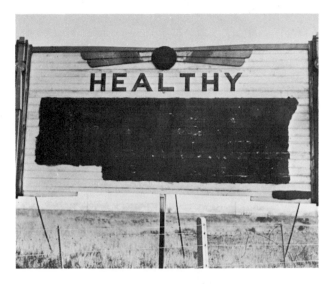

HEALTHY

Overnight it had become a respectable and patriotic way of travelling ... even for girls. The need for conscience and coercion in reducing petrol consumption was confirmed by statistics: a single Lancaster needed two thousand gallons of petrol to reach the Ruhr.

When you got to the Ruhr at least you knew you were there, but there were often grave doubts as to where you were in Britain with sign-posts and station signs blotted out, railway stations blacked out and bus stops drastically reduced. The blackout made many journeys into adventures, most of which you would have avoided if you could. Yet there could be a strong sense of willing comradeship in the carriage or even the corridor.

What you saw on the roads or on the railways – if you could see anything – was often strange: buses and cars with gas bags on the roof or pulling cylinders full of producer gas; eight-foot-wide trolley-buses, designed for Durban and Johannesburg, in Barking and Ilford; 'Wild-West' style locomotives manned by Negro crews in places as unlikely as the New Forest; debutantes and other celebrities pedalling patriotically around town on bicycles; doctors and clergymen visiting their patients and parishioners on horseback. But the least strange and the most available form of transport was Shanks's pony. The government recommended it for getting to work and pleasure. If you actually got around and took a holiday it was as likely as not to be a hiking holiday. The open spaces seemed far away from all the hardship and danger of the cities – the abiding England that (as we shall see) could never quite be fenced in.

ROAD CLOSED

'They can't blackout the moon'

(1939 song title)

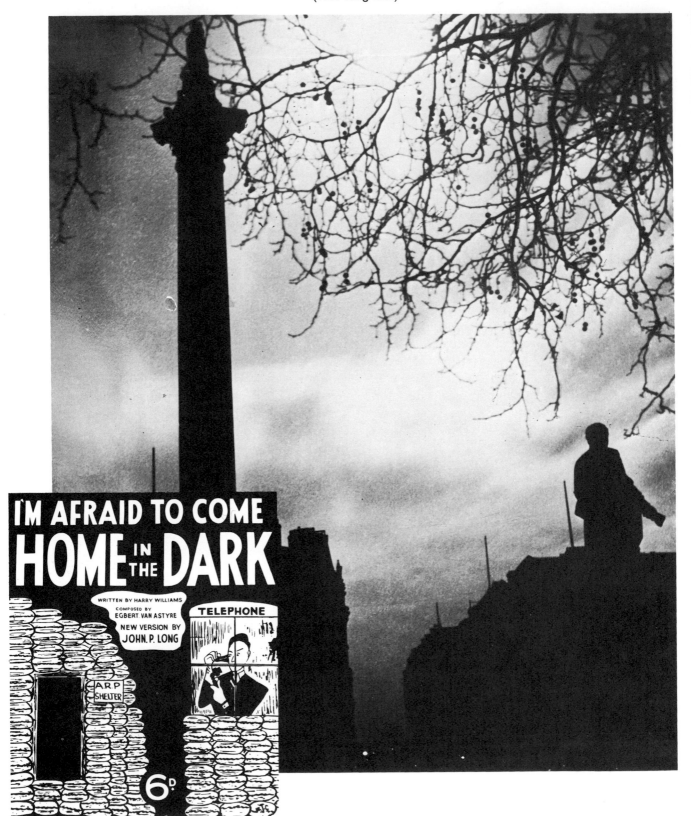

'Moonlight becomes you'

(1942 song title)

At the beginning of the war the blackout was extolled by lovers and aesthetes. 'London – the new Rome: Moonlight scenes of mystic calm,' rhapsodized the *Illustrated London News* in October 1939 above photographs which, they claimed, 'reveal the unsuspected unappreciated architectural splendours of buildings wholly classical in the calm purity of their outlines'. At the end of the war *Vogue*, in an article on 'What we want to keep from the war', suggested 'The blackout, one night a year, a night of full moon, to remind us of its beauty.' For most people, however, the blackout was a source of jokes, songs and grumbles, a cause of wasting time, getting lost and getting hurt, whilst moonlight, the dreaded 'Bomber's Moon', meant not beauty but danger.

To help passengers in the blackout the numbers on London trams were transferred from the top front to the side to enable them to be illuminated legally (*left*). A more general blackout aid was the Government's decree in 1940 that 'Summer Time should start in February.' (It was retained throughout the war, annually supplemented during the actual summer months by 'Double Summer Time'.)

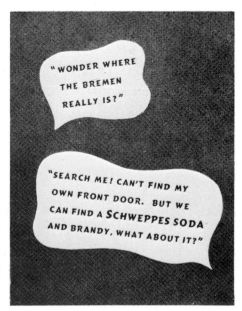

"WONDER WHERE THE BREMEN REALLY IS?"

"SEARCH ME! CAN'T FIND MY OWN FRONT DOOR. BUT WE CAN FIND A SCHWEPPES SODA AND BRANDY. WHAT ABOUT IT?"

'Blackout - Carry a White Pekinese'

(Advertisement in the *Daily Telegraph*)

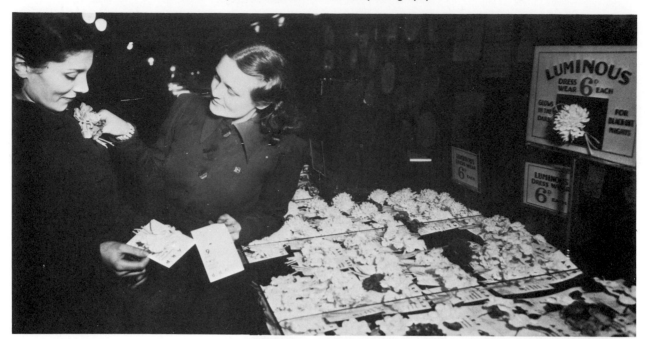

'*Everybody do the "Black-out Stroll"
Laugh and drive your cares right up the
     pole.*'
(*Right*) A couple takes the advice of the
song.
A wide range of luminous haberdashery
was on sale from walking sticks and dog
collars to armbands and artificial flowers
(*above*). In October 1939 the *Observer*
reported that 'Marshall and Snelgrove
are having a great success with their
blackout coats for dogs. Costing half a
guinea, they are made in white gleaming
fabric (with an occasional red spot) . . .
with bells to announce his coming. Add,
too, your dog's identity disc, and even if
he should stray, you can feel that he is
safe.' Some difficulties were less soluble:
Reynolds News reported in January 1940
that 'West End solicitors, who before
the war netted five figure incomes from
divorce cases, have been heavily hit by
the blackout. In the winter months at
any rate, private inquiry agents are
helpless. Adultery cannot be proved
because identification is impossible in the
pitch dark.'

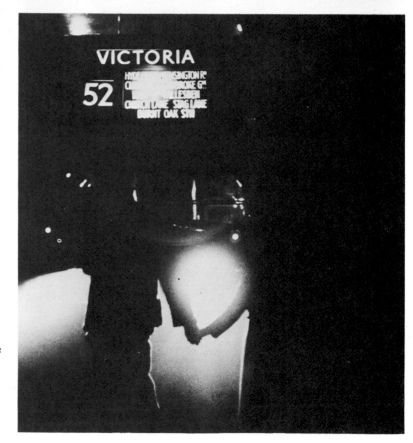

'The world's most exemplary passenger . . .'

Billy's Bulletin

No. ABB 1234 THIS YEAR, NEXT YEAR A CRUSADE FOR WISER TRAVEL PRICELESS

All the Browns (and Brownes) Agree—
LOOK OUT IN THE BLACK-OUT IS THE BEST POLICY

WHEN Billy Brown goes out at night he wears or carries something white. When Mrs. Brown is in the black-out she likes to wear her old white mack out.

And Sally Brown straps round her shoulder a natty plain white knick-knack holder.

. . so they may be seen at night

The reason why they wear this white is so they may be seen at night.

Down below the station's bright, but here outside it's black as night. Billy Brown will wait a bit and let his eyes grow used to it. Then he'll scan the road and see.

before he crosses, if it's free; remembering when lights are dim that cars he sees may not see him.

The safest travelling in town is not too good for Billy Brown. He's much too sensible and knowing to jump down off a bus that's going, especially in black-out hours, or when the kerb is wet with showers. On these occasions Billy B. goes by the slogan 'Wait and See.'

Cars he sees may not see him

His slogan : Wait and See.

PATTERN SHOPPER

'YOU see, my dear', said Billy Brown, 'how transport services in town begin their main rush-hours by 4 (much earlier than before the war). And so, when shopping it's my view that you, and other shoppers too, should try to start for home by 3.' 'I will, my dear', said Mrs. B.

For copper rides, says Billy Brown,
I never tender half-a-crown :
The right amount saves much delay
And speeds the tram upon its way

No Jam

NOT for our hero, anyhow. Not the sort of jam that spills out of a bottle-neck of overflowing traffic. But read on.

Billy finds it quite a strain to get himself inside a train : with such a squash around the door there's hardly room for any more. But down the car there's heaps of space and everyone could find a place. 'So let's all move along', says Billy : 'to crowd the entrance up is silly.'

Many or few, it's
BETTER TO QUEUE

BILLY'S standing in a queue, as we all must sometimes do. Queueing in these days of rush means you don't have any crush, and the seconds saved will lend extra wings to journey's end. But, says Billy, see you choose the proper one of several queues!

Today's
GOOD Deed

WHEN you travel to and fro, on a line you really know, remember those who aren't so sure and haven't been that way before. Do your good deed for the day — tell them the stations on the way.

WHAT'S IN A NAME ?

THE answer is Everything—if you use it to good purpose, as Billy Brown does.

QUIZ CORNER Says Billy Brown, 'It seems to me that things get lost quite needlessly. Because they bear no name inside they cannot be identified. My name and address are found on everything I take around, and so I'm very pleased to see you think it wise to copy me.'

Billy Brown has had a rise in bus men's estimation
Since he paid the fare exact and named his destination

Billy Brown's Own Highway Code—

He flags his bus with something white

for black-outs is 'Stay off the Road'. He'll never step out and begin to meet a bus that's pulling in. He doesn't wave his torch at night, but 'flags' his bus with something white. He never jostles in a queue, but waits and takes his turn—
Do you ?

That's the Stuff (It may Save YOUR LIFE)

IN the train a fellow sits and pulls the window-net to bits, because the view is somewhat dim, a fact which seems to worry him.

As Billy cannot bear the sight, he says 'My man, that is not right. I trust you'll pardon my correction: That stuff is there for your protection.'

THE WORLD'S MOST EXEMPLARY PASSENGER

When travelling on the Underground, you must have noticed, I'll be bound, little notes of friendly warning which one looks at every morning, referring to a Billy Brown, a citizen of London Town—a bloke who always does things right, a chap whose torch is not too bright, who scans his black-out every night, won't drive a car if he gets tight . . .

Now Billy, I have heard it said, would shake a disapproving head at those who never can refrain from scratching at the window pane. A glance would say, in their direction, 'This is here for your protection.' Of netted glass we see about the same is true, without a doubt. A time may come amidst the strife, when covered windows save a life . . . . .

Let us, then, not be forgetting of this, our duty to the netting.

Face the driver · · · ·
Face the driver · · · ·

Hail your bus or tram in the correct way.

Do you use the
BB Sign ?

Face the driver, raise you hand—
You'll find that he will understand

STOP PRESS

'No Smoking' Rule Breach
Significant Incident

At Bow Street Police Court to-day Billy Brown was commended by magistrate for frustrating attempt by passenger on Underground to smoke in car labelled 'No Smoking.'

'Is your Journey Really Necessary?'

Some didactic posters retained a First-World-War style (*right*). The artist was Bert Thomas, who drew 'Ole Bill' in the 1914–18 war. This new Tommy is too close a relative. The extreme discomfort of wartime railway journeys ensured that few people travelled unless their journey *was* really necessary. In the *Observer* 'Observator' commented grandly in February 1940 that 'the discontinuance of first class on the Underground is only one of several jolts to the social code which the war is giving us. Not that it matters: we can all afford to be a little more democratic for a few months, just as we change our clocks every year in the same cause.'

RAILWAY EXECUTIVE COMMITTEE

"... Now, if it means 'Is your journey really NECESSARY?' then the answer's Yes, and I want a third return to Morecambe Bay—but if it means 'Is your journey REALLY necessary?' then I merely want a single back to Pinner."

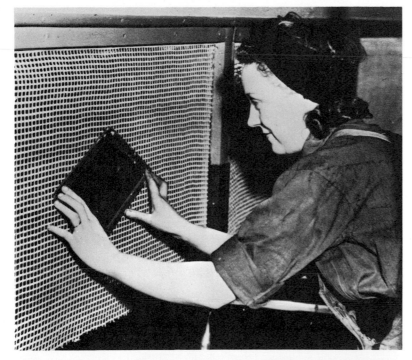

We should have gone by bus for the child's sake.

Girl in blacked-out train: 'Take your hand off my knee! Not you, you!'

Woman in train during raid: 'Oh Christ, I wish I was aht of this train.'
Man: 'Don't you worry, me gel! You couldn't be in a safer place – safe as 'ouses. They carn't 'it a moving target.'

The windows of tube trains (*above and above left*) were covered to protect passengers from flying glass if the windows were broken by bomb-blast. Harold Nicolson wrote in his diary in July 1945, 'Meanwhile all the sticky stuff has been removed from the windows of the buses and undergrounds, and we shall no longer remember how we used to peep out through a little diamond slit in the texture to read the names of the stations as they flashed by. One forgets these things at once.'

'See that the Enemy gets no Petrol'

(Government leaflet, *If the Invader Comes*, 1940)

Petrol rationing which started on 22 September 1939 produced an instant – and lasting – boom in cycling, with *The Times* reporting 'an exceptional demand by well-to-do people for machines'. The *New Yorker* reported that 'cycles are appearing in the streets in increasing quantities, ridden by young girls in slacks, by civil servants pedalling down to Whitehall, and by smart women, trimly snooded and headed for lunch at the Berkeley'. (*Right*) Girls of the ARP 'Bike Wheel Brigade' being inspected at a Clapham factory.

Garage owners faced strange new difficulties: 'Retired barrister or KC. Situation offered for "duration", charge of two petrol pumps and coupons. Whole-time job. Average intelligence essential.' (Advertisement in situations column of the *Garage and Motor Agent*, December 1941)

They also had to adapt to changing circumstances. (*Above*) A 'pool' petrol pump in the south of England drained as an anti-invasion precaution.

'Stepping on the gas'

Cycling was not the only way of saving petrol, but it was difficult to step on the gas when it was balanced on the roof of your car or van, housed in an unwieldy balloon resting on a wooden frame. The balloon held ordinary unrationed town gas, the equivalent of one gallon of petrol, and a network of supply-points ten miles apart was set up in the London area. After 1942 the fuel shortage led to the end of such conversions, and the withdrawal of existing ones.

For some customers there was always enough petrol (*below and below left*).

"Do you play bridge?"

'Go by Shanks' pony' . . . or a real one

"Funny thing, I can always tell when the sirens have sounded."

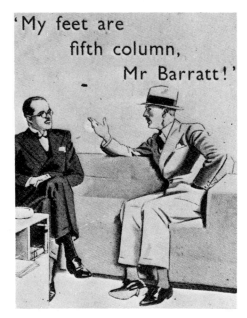

'My feet are fifth column, Mr Barratt!'

In 1940 nine out of ten families did not own a car. Many of them took the Government's advice (*right*) and 'walked short distances'. Others preferred horseback. All sorts of riding horses and ponies as well as cart and ploughing horses were in demand again at rapidly rising prices. During air raids in cities drivers of delivery carts were advised to unharness their horses and tether them to the back of the cart to prevent bolting (*above* and *above right*).

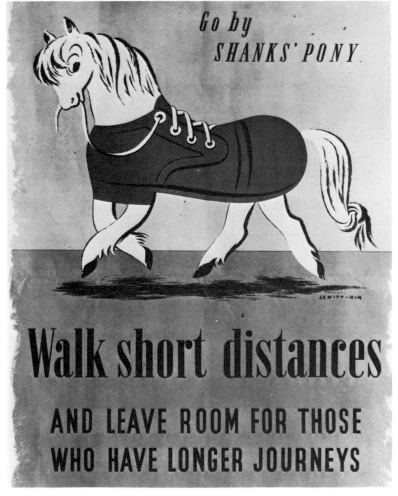

Go by SHANKS' PONY

Walk short distances
AND LEAVE ROOM FOR THOSE WHO HAVE LONGER JOURNEYS

The rule of the raid

in a raid—

Motorists-park your car close to the kerb off the main highway. *AT NIGHT*, switch off head lamp. Keep side and rear lights on

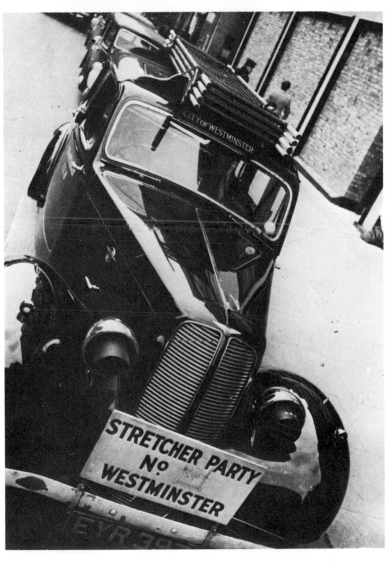

Wartime vehicles had to be as adaptable as travellers. They had to abide by the rule of the raid (*above*) as well as the rule of the road. Some cars (*left*) joined the ambulance service and many buses were converted into emergency ambulances. Many London taxis became auxiliary fire engines and pulled trailer pumps, whilst lorries often took the place of buses in helping people to get to work. Whatever they were they had to be equipped with headlight masks of an official design (*left*) (obligatory from January 1940 after months of makeshift experiments with old socks and tissue paper. Only one headlamp could be lit, the bulb being removed from the other). The masks and the lack of signposts combined to make every journey a mystery tour: the most sensible traveller was the one who stayed at – or near – home. As *Vogue* put it: 'Always hospitable, people in the country now fall upon casual visitors with open arms, for what with the lack of petrol and the black-out, they are forced to stay at home and seldom see what in peacetime would be comparatively close neighbours.'

'Somewhere in England'

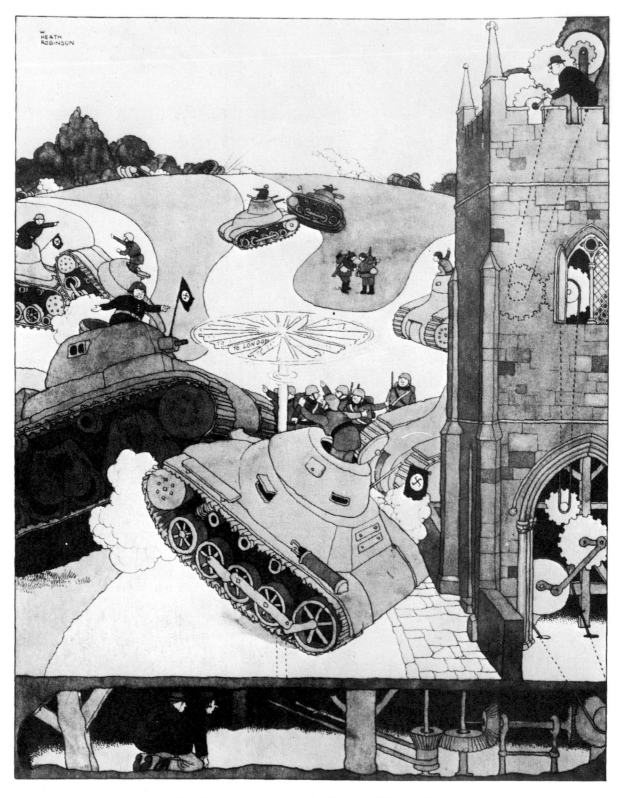

Confusing the Enemy's Sense of Direction

Signs of the times

In June 1940 life became even more difficult for the motorist. With the fear of imminent invasion came the Government's order that 'no person shall display or cause or permit to be displayed any sign which furnishes any indication of the name of, or the situation or the direction of, or the distance to any place'. Station signs disappeared; signposts were uprooted (*below*) all tell-tale evidence of whereabouts was removed. An AA scout (*left*) strips a box of its direction signs and blacks out the name. Anthony Eden, Secretary of State for War, broadcast to 'those of you who are not in the Forces': 'Stay where you are! Refugees on roads or railways hamstring those upon whom your defence depends . . . The mass of refugees helped to lose the battle of France; they will not lose the battle of Britain.'

125

Goodbye to joy-rides . . .

(Above) *Italian Prisoners-of-War Working on the Land* by Michael Ford.

(Below) *Foreign Servicemen in Hyde Park: Early Summer, 1940* by Kenneth Rowntree.

Getting Together

A Christmas party for the Allies in London, 1942.

OVER THERE

"*Dear Momma, in England they drive on the left side of the road . . .*"

Over there, over there,
Send the word, send the word over there,
The Yanks are coming, the Yanks are coming,
Drum, drum, drumming everywhere.

'Wild West style' locomotives manned by negro crews were only one exotic symbol of the new kind of interdependence which brightened wartime ways of life. Nylon stockings were another – described austerely as 'the best wearing stockings in the world', but thought of also (when so many legs went bare) as 'magic garments'. There were reports from the United States, from which so many blessings flowed, of the miracles of modern science being applied not to radar or to rocketry but to making coats out of chemicals.

Every American camp in Britain carried with it a touch of American glamour, even a shade of Hollywood. So, too, of course, did Rainbow Corner – appropriately named – just off Piccadilly Circus. The Club there sold only soft drinks (ten thousand were sold there in a week) but it kept special bunks for those GIs who had 'lost a bout with British beer'. Many of the American objects themselves seemed as exciting as the GIs. The long cartons of Lucky Strike and Camels, for example, which had seldom been seen in Britain before 1939, looked as if they had appeared not out of the PX but out of an Aladdin's cave. So, too, did American stores, complete with ice-cream, canned tomato juice, doughnuts and peanut butter.

Attitudes were mixed on both sides. The Americans could never accept 'medieval' English heating and plumbing. Yet many, at least, felt that Britain had a touch of glamour too, in places like Edinburgh and Oxford, and even London, which everyone said looked 'drab' before they arrived, quickly proved itself 'the best leave town of the war'. The oldest among them felt that our 'over there' had not changed very much in some places since the First World War (Piccadilly, Leicester Square and all that) when the song 'Over There' had been written and marched to. The song immediately became a hit again after Pearl Harbor like scores of other American songs.

The first Americans landed in January 1942 not in England or Scotland, but in Ulster. Their arrival, the London *New Yorker* correspondent told her readers, cheered people enormously, not least the Canadian troops who were hopeful that the new garrison would eventually release some of them for action. There had been large numbers of Canadians in Britain, of course, since the First Canadian Division had landed at Greenock on 17 December 1939 along with Australians, New Zealanders and Poles, Norwegians and even a few Americans of the Tyrone Power 'Yank in the RAF' vintage. The Canadian Charles Ritchie noted on Christmas Day, 1940 how he had watched at a country station 'bold-eyed Canadians – with a slouch and a swagger, New Zealanders with overcoats hanging untidily, Australians often with girls, and English soldiers going back to London saying goodbye to plain, loyal wives wearing spectacles and sometimes carrying babies.'

There were British stereotypes – sometimes class stereotypes too – for all the first visiting troops. The Poles looked as if they had walked off an opera set, the Norwegians as if they had just made their way from the Arctic frosts (as often they had). From May 1940 onwards the range of stereotypes was extended as living in England – to quote again the *New Yorker*'s correspondent – came to resemble living on 'a vast combination of an aircraft carrier, a floating dock jammed with men and a warehouse stacked to the ceiling with material labelled "Europe"'.

The Belgians were brave but 'betrayed by their King' (so unlike 1914) and the Dutch honest, solid and thoroughly reliable, but the French seemed to have brought France (including its quarrels) across the Channel with them to Britain. French soldiers and sailors were French and 'free', and there was a wartime joke that all London's prostitutes (though they were neither French nor free) claimed to belong to them.

Most of the national stereotypes, starting with the Poles, involved sex and there was certainly never any shortage of girls at Rainbow Corner. Throughout the country there was no shortage of brides either, and it was a sign of the times in the last year of the war that the Federation of American Women's Clubs presented fifty satin bridal dresses (complete with veils and orange blossom) to be hired out at ten shillings a time to new British service brides. The brides of Canadian soldiers actually formed a club in Sussex (which had become a great Canadian centre) under the guidance of the mayoress of Brighton in order to learn about Canada before they arrived there.

"This is our Bridal Suite."

Civilian refugees and officials of emigré governments always attracted less attention than soldiers, sailors and airmen, glamorous or otherwise, although in their case they introduced to London a whiff not only of Paris or Brussels or Amsterdam but of Geneva. News stalls were thick with foreign journals, some with unpronounceable Czech or Polish names, each with its own slant, and often sharply contradictory. And Allied nationals were employed in large numbers in British war work, not least the BBC. For many broadcasters Bush House was the real centre of BBC operations, not Broadcasting House, and some of the teams of foreigners had a remarkable measure of political and artistic independence.

It was from BBC studios also that the American correspondents (the first of their compatriots to travel 'over there') broadcast back across the Atlantic long before the United States came into the war and Ed Murrow and Dorothy Thompson both became household names.

The British Ambassador in Washington was at pains, too, to stress from the outset that 'it was very desirable' that 'the Americans should be given the truth about what was happening', whatever it was.

The closest contact most Americans had with war before Pearl Harbor was through Canada, though it was a country at war with no blackouts or bombs and with a prime minister, Mackenzie King, whose views on war (and Britain) were ambivalent. In the spring of 1939 King had attacked what he called 'the idea that every twenty years this country should automatically and as a matter of course take part in a war overseas, periodically, to fight for a continent that cannot run itself'. Yet he was to try to establish 'spirit links' with Canada's prime minister in the First World War and to go on to write a book called *Canada at Britain's Side*.

In 1940 an American journalist quoted a Canadian who said that 'we are at war with Germany yet we could not win a war against the State of Michigan'. Yet by 1942 three hundred thousand Canadians had enrolled in Canada's Navy, Army and Air Force, and the Canadian war effort (drawing upon forty per cent of the national income) was rightly described as 'herculean'. There was never any doubt about the desire of the Canadian troops to fight or of the determination of the staff of the Canadian High Commission in London to galvanize the war effort.

Australians and New Zealanders were notoriously tough fighters also, and *Melody Maker*, with one eye on North Africa, noted how the Australian song 'Waltzing Matilda' became a smash hit in London in 1941. 'The Australians left Sydney singing "Waltzing Matilda". They arrived in Egypt singing "Waltzing Matilda". They captured Bardia singing "Waltzing Matilda".'

The Germans did their best in their divisive target propaganda to prove that 'Britain fought to the last Canadian ... or Frenchman or Dutchman or Greek' and, before America entered the war, to exploit the argument that 'England expects every

American to do his duty'. Yet the desire to fight on the part of all Britain's Allies needed no British prompting, Machiavellian or otherwise. There was a greater danger to inter-Allied relations, popular and official, between 1940 and 1944 in that many of them had to wait impatiently in these islands rather than fight . . . with the Americans among the troops waiting in the second half of this period.

Official links between Britain and the United States had never been so close as they ought to have been before 1939 and unofficial links were almost as limited. The war multiplied all kinds of links before Pearl Harbor, even before the Atlantic Charter. On 31 May 1941 the first consignment of food for civilians under Lend Lease arrived at a British port – four million eggs, 120,000 pounds of cheese and one thousand tons of flour – to be received officially by Lord Woolton, the Minister of Food, and Averell Harriman who, as the President's personal representative, was in charge of Lend Lease operations in London. (A twenty-pound cheese was distributed among the unloading staff of two hundred and forty dockers.)

It was not only national bulk buying – even on credit – which provided an obvious new link between civilians across the Atlantic. Thousands of private food parcels were also sent as gifts. And even these were only part of the free flow of assistance. War nurseries in Britain were equipped almost entirely with American help. Thus, from Kettering, a WVS officer wrote to the United States describing how, in her local nursery 'all the tables and chairs had been given by America . . . all the beds the children rested on in the afternoons, all the cutlery and the crockery and all the cooking equipment'. As the teacher-in-charge summed it up, 'America gave it all.'

The Atlantic Charter, with its forward look at a world free from 'the Nazi tyranny' was described grandiloquently at the time as a document which ranked with Magna Carta and the Declaration of Independence, and if Japanese deeds at Pearl Harbor eventually counted for more than words, however eloquent, wartime partnership between Britain and the United States had been prepared long before. None the less, the first American troops, it was felt, required very special advice when they reached the shores of Britain. Every GI received a booklet warning him of all the possible pitfalls – in the language so deceptively shared and in the culture.

'The British are often more reserved in conduct than we,' and 'You can rub a Britisher the wrong way by telling him "We came over and won the last one."' The British were given advice also – in articles, even in sermons. 'Remember everything is twice as much fun to these American boys if there's a girl in it.' 'Don't let the warmth of your welcome extend to your drinks.' 'People get along best with their own sort and many will be happier in your gardener's cottage than in your house.' Many Britons responded and an American wartime article called 'When GI Joes Took London' noted that the Red Cross alone had dealt with seventy-five thousand invitations from 'Britishers' asking 'our boys' to their homes. The Americans were often happiest in the remotest places where no foreigner had ever set foot before – in villages near lonely aerodromes or in billets in small provincial towns. 'Reports are now coming in from the country', wrote Mollie Panter-Downes in 1942, 'as to how our boys are settling down with the natives. In one village the elderly and autocratic lady of the manor overheard herself described by her guests as "a swell old guy". She was as delighted as if the President had sent her a decoration.'

The visit to Britain of the American President's wife, Eleanor Roosevelt, in October 1942 – everyone was at pains to point out that as President's wife she had 'no official status' – was one of the highlights of the social history of the war. Mrs Roosevelt listened as much as she talked, taking care to meet not only 'leaders' but what she called 'the rank and file'.

It was certainly through the rank and file that the most important cultural contacts of the war took place – most of them, like the fascinating encounter between people in this country and American Negro troops, unexplored by anthropologists (except for the ever-curious and ever-zealous Mass Observation). When a vicar's wife in Worle, near Weston-Super-Mare (she was obviously no Eleanor Roosevelt) told her husband's parishioners that if a local woman kept a shop and a coloured soldier entered she must serve him but 'must do it as quickly as possible and indicate that she does not desire him to come there again', the *Sunday Pictorial* retorted that all black Americans should be assured that 'there is no colour bar in this country' and that 'the vast majority of people here have nothing but repugnance for the narrow-minded, uninformed prejudices expressed by the vicar's wife'.

Fortunately, although race relations created some problems, there were plenty of good English girls who would have instantly dismissed the second admonition of the vicar's wife that 'if a woman is in a cinema and notices a coloured soldier next to her, she should move to another seat immediately'. Not very far from Weston-Super-Mare, Wellington was described by a Somerset housewife in August 1942 as being 'a seething mass of darkies now, followed by children who can't leave them alone ... Our local girls are much attracted and Dobbie's foreman saw three at the camp gate, looking longingly in. "They maids – prick-mazed they be, prick-mazed" was his comment.'

Prisoners of war – particularly the Italians – could inspire not dissimilar feelings. For the Italians to be 'over here' was really to be 'fenced in', even if they were in the open fields. Yet there was ample scope for fraternizing (despite an unsuccessful campaign in the popular newspapers in 1941 against the employment of Italian prisoners on farms). 'Italian prisoners were ditching a field,' Kingsley Martin reported in the *New Statesman* in January 1942. 'A guard supervised their unenergetic labours. He was there to see that they did not escape, not to encourage them to toil. "How do you get on with your Wops?" asked the next door farmer, over the hedge. The soldier grinned broadly. "Man," he said, "there's nae pairt o' Italy that I havenae been invited tae!"'

There was a marked contrast between attitudes to Italian prisoners of war (some of whom found their own brides) and the foreign 'enemy' refugees, most of them dedicated anti-Nazis, who had been rounded up ignominiously in the summer of 1940 and sent 'over there' to the Isle of Man.

Ideology had little to do with popular likes and dislikes. Neither did talk – either of a future Atlantic Union or of a United Europe. The BBC's V . . . _ campaign of the spring and summer of 1941, which started before Russia – let alone the United States – entered the war, appealed, through 'voices in the darkness' to unseen national resistance movements in different European countries (Britain's abandoned 'over there'), but it was premature and as out-of-touch with operational realities as was an advertisement in the *Berkeley and Sharpness Gazette* in February 1941: 'Learn French, Italian, German for controlling subjugated enemies after the war. Very good pronunciation. Easily taught by – – –.' 'Colonel Britton' (Douglas Ritchie) dreamed of 'the co-ordination of resistance' in an 'underground army' before Europe and the British were ready for it. It was only after there had been what seemed to be interminable delays in opening up a Second Front to help the Russians that Europe became 'over there' on D-Day, 6 June 1944, an Allied operation in which all (including a huffy de Gaulle) took part.

Seven hundred and twenty-five out of 914 American radio stations carried BBC programmes on that day, reporting back what was happening in Normandy, and on the new SHAEF radio station, which started broadcasting the day after D-Day; British and American voices alternated in reading the special message from General Eisenhower to the Allied troops. An American Army chaplain said the first prayer, and American, Canadian and British announcers read the news in turn to maintain 'parity', if not 'purity', of expression. 'If this isn't inter-Allied co-operation', a British major commented, 'I don't know what it is – unless it's murder.'

By then, of course, London was 'over there' again, and the capitals to be reached by the Allies were Paris, Brussels, the Hague – and Berlin.

LEADERS OF THE ALLIED NATIONS WHOSE HEADQUARTERS ARE IN BRITAIN

. be backing a quitter' (Lord Lothian, British Ambassador in Washington, 1940)

"*You'll see a few changes, Sir, since them Canadians moved in.*"

'You burned the city of London in our houses and we felt the flames that burned it. You laid the dead of London at our doors and we knew the dead were our dead – were all men's dead – were mankind's dead – and ours', wrote American poet Archibald MacLeish to the great American broadcaster, Ed Murrow, who ('brave, resourceful, superbly articulate') broadcast regularly from Britain to his fellow countrymen.

'If they can't get a fight soon they will take England to pieces to see what makes it tick!' wrote F. Tennyson Jesse in July 1940 of the thousands of restless foreign and Dominion servicemen 'cooped up in Britain waiting for action'. (*Top left*) *Polish Soldiers* by Feliks Topolski.

'You ally. You ally!'

(Chant of Norwegian 'specials' reported by Norman Longmate)

'Refugees are beginning to arrive from the Continent – tough-looking Norwegian seamen with shocks of coarse blond hair, dressed in blue serge suits, lunching at Garland's Hotel – Dutch peasant girls in native costume like coloured photographs in the *Geographical Magazine* – walking down Cockspur Street carrying their worldly possessions tied up in bundles. A group of Dutch soldiers in the street in German-looking uniforms gives one a turn. (Shall we see German soldiers in London streets?)' (Charles Ritchie, *The Siren Years*, diary for May 1940) Allies strong and weak: a Polish serviceman (*right*) and a Belgian refugee, 1940 (*below*).

The Poles in their glamorous uniforms often seemed the most exciting to the girls, especially when they possessed special talents.

Italy entered the war against the Allies on 10 June 1940, cynically waiting until Hitler's victory in Europe seemed certain. 'What a mean skulking thing to do . . . They are like the people who rob corpses on the battlefield,' wrote Harold Nicolson in his diary, whilst the *New Statesman*'s editorial the following week was headed simply 'Enter the Second Murderer'. Yet laughter was the typical reaction to Italy's entrance into the war, partly, no doubt (as Kingsley Martin wrote) because 'owing to a silly British convention Italy suggests macaroni and ice cream and is funny in itself like beer and Wigan'. (15 June 1940)

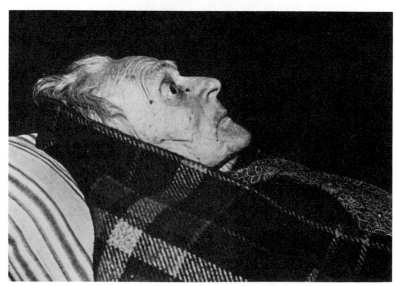

'Oh! What a surprise for the Duce'

(Title of popular song written when Mussolini was beaten by the Greeks)

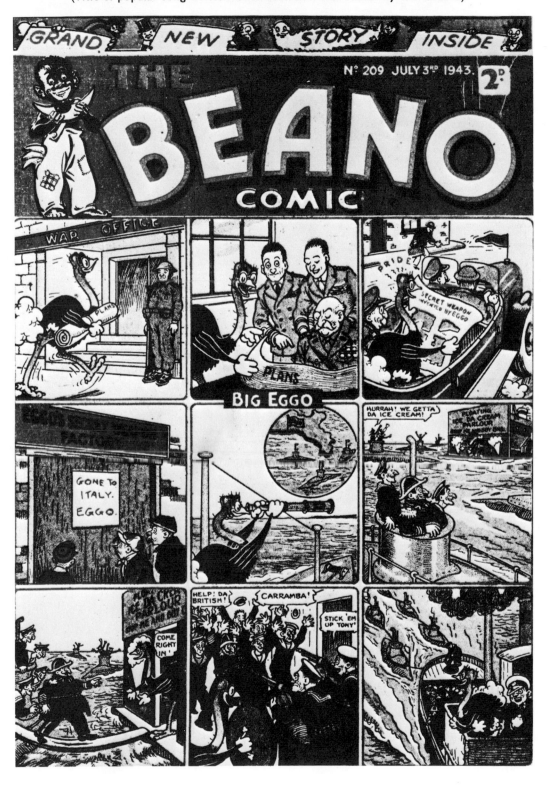

First they came . . . and then

Edward Ardizzone's watercolour of the arrival of the first American troops in Ulster, January 1942 (*right*). The French were already here (*below*). In 1940 thousands of French troops arrived in Britain, among them ten thousand sailors. For General de Gaulle France had lost a battle but had not lost the war: 'Les mêmes moyens qui nous ont vaincus peuvent nous donner un jour la victoire.'

'She walked me off my feet'

(*Daily Mail* reporter covering Mrs Roosevelt's visit to Britain)

'I thought you would like to know Mrs Roosevelt's visit here is a great success. She has been very happy about it herself. I hope that the friendly reception by all people here has been reported as enthusiastically at home as it has been in this country. If you have any suggestions I will be glad to follow them.' (Churchill in a cable to President Roosevelt, October 1942)

BBC reporter (Stewart MacPherson) to passer-by in street interview: 'Have you seen Mrs Roosevelt since she has been in London?'
Passer-by: 'No, but I understand that her chief purpose in coming here is to have intercourse with the American troops.' (Quoted by Gilbert Harding in his autobiography, *Along My Line*)

'Over-paid, Over-sexed, and Over here!'

In September 1942 James Agate described a conversation with two young American airmen newly-arrived in England. One of them leaned over to me and said, 'Say, buddy, d'ya think we could take a coupla women to our hotel?' I asked what hotel they were staying at, and he mentioned one of the most respectable hostelries in London. I told him they could not possibly do such a thing. 'Aw', says airman No. 2, 'don't get us wrong. We don't mean a coupla women each!'

In late 1942 *Vogue* reported that 'people are talking about the gay American negro troops (not troupes) and the possibility of the arrival of coloured WAACs'.

'The first coloured service girls get down to work in Britain,' was the ambiguous contemporary caption to this photograph (*below right*), London 1943.

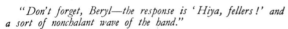
"*Don't forget, Beryl—the response is 'Hiya, fellers!' and a sort of nonchalant wave of the hand.*"

'Boy meets Girl'

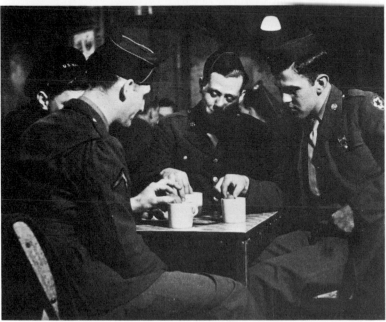

'We shall remember Piccadilly Circus after dark . . . the swarms of people, the fifty different uniforms . . . the girl who sang operatic arias on the Bakerloo platform as everyone cheered . . . the sailor who played his violin and danced in the Morden train when everyone joined in "*Dear Liverpool*".' (From a letter written by a young American soldier before D-Day in case he never came back)

After D-Day London emptied and the gaiety and the sense of pressure and excitement vanished, but some of the fraternizing lasted: US Army postal officials found that one letter in eight posted from American beachheads in Normandy went to friends and sweethearts in England.

'Glenn Miller is missing'

(Headline of *Melody Maker*, 30 December 1944)

When Major Glenn Miller came to England in July 1944 with the American band of the Allied Expeditionary Force – 48 strong – his band, to quote *Melody Maker*, immediately 'rocketed to the peak of British affection by their impeccable playing and brilliant musicianship, as well as the polished slickness with which their broadcasts and concerts are carried out'. Miller's plane vanished on a journey to Paris and he was announced missing on Christmas Eve 1944, never to be seen again.

'Titling these shows is important,' said the producer of many smash-hit American shows, like *Stage-Door Canteen*, 1944 (*right*). 'They must have the GI slant.'

'Coney Island in Piccadilly'

The Amusement Caterers Association presented these pin tables from the piers and promenades of closed-down holiday resorts to Rainbow Corner in 1942. They were worked free of charge with prizes of American candy and cigarettes.

'The Yanks are coming . . . so beware'

(Line from song 'Over There')

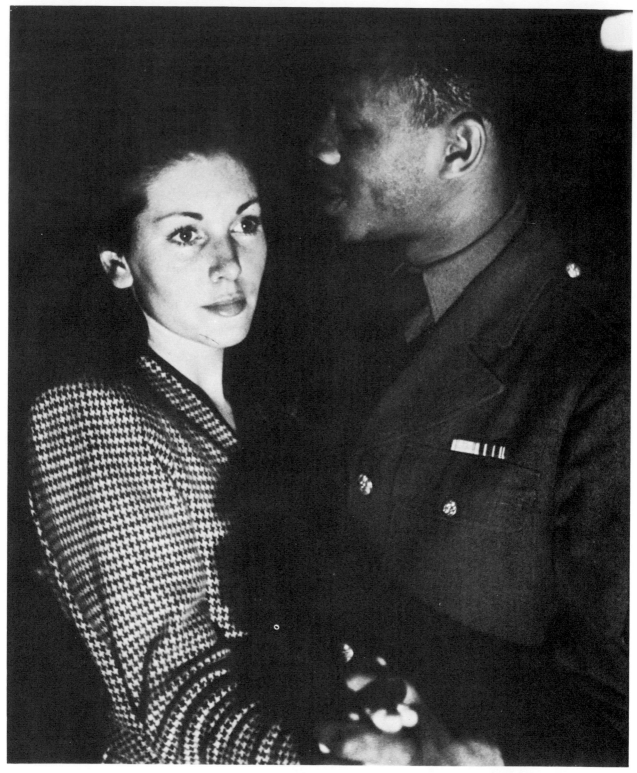

'. . . for a white woman to go about in the company of a Negro American is likely to lead to controversy and ill-feeling. It may also be misunderstood by the Negro troops themselves.' (Extract from the Government's 'Instructions as to the advice which should be given to British Service Personnel', 1942)

'Got any gum, chum?'

"Quite *a little evening ceremony—Earl and Chester make Edwin a cup of tea and he makes* them *a mint-julep.*"

'But we shall remember, too, our Christmas parties for the orphans and the evacuees. No one could ever forget those parties, with the kids yelling and gobbling ice-cream, sitting on our shoulders and singing for us. Fifteen hundred we had at one party.' (Extract from a GI letter, 1944)

Instead of spending Thanksgiving 1942 in the traditional 'enjoy yourselves' way, members of the US 8th Air Force gave a party for two hundred British war orphans at their headquarters (*left centre*). The children's mouths were open not just for the food but to sing 'Pack up your Troubles' for a broadcast to America.

Extract from the booklet prepared by the US War Department and issued to every American soldier entering our country as a wartime guest: 'Britain may look a little shop-worn and grimy to you. There's been a war on since 1939. The houses haven't been painted, because factories are not making paint – they're making planes. British trains are cold because power is used for industry, not for heating. The British people are anxious for you to know that in normal times Britain looks much prettier, cleaner, neater. Don't be misled by the British tendency to be soft-spoken and polite. They can be plenty tough, too. The English language didn't spread across the oceans, mountains, jungles and swamps of the world because these people were "panty-waists". Remember that crossing the ocean doesn't automatically make you a hero. There are housewives in aprons and youngsters in knee pants who have lived through more high explosives than many soldiers saw in the last war. If your British host exhorts you to "eat up – there's plenty on the table", go easy – it might be the family's ration for a week, spread out to show their hospitality.'

'Give us the tools and we will finish the job'

(Churchill in a broadcast to America in February 1941)

A month after Churchill's broadcast, Roosevelt's Lend-Lease Act gave him power to give Britain almost limitless aid. Not only tools, but huge shipments of food – dried eggs, bacon, beans, tinned meat – poured into the country. Gifts of clothing from overseas had been arriving since the beginning of the war, often personally marked with the donor's name . . . (see label *above left*) . . . and the WVS became a universal provider.

In September 1940, when the raids on London and other parts of the country had begun, the American Red Cross – only one of the donors – asked WVS to spend £84,000 on their behalf to provide necessities for people who had been bombed, and some of this money was spent on clothing and blankets. Subsequently WVS received from them 10,848,321 new garments, 245,232 layettes, 819,126 blankets and 832,235 pairs of boots and shoes . . . Most of what was left over in 1945 was used in liberated countries. A WVS report from a Camberwell clothing depot after a raid described a child 'dressed by kindness from all over the world. I never noticed at the time, but we put her into a skirt from Australia, a pullover from a work party in Ontario, her shoes were American and her coat a present from a New Zealand school.'

(*Below right*) Wendell Wilkie, Roosevelt's Republican rival in 1940 arrived in Britain during the Blitz and was just as impressed by the British war effort and spirit as Roosevelt himself. Wilkie's dream was already 'one world'.

" I LIKE THEIR NERVE "

HEY LITTLE HEN!

"How would you like your egg this month, dear?"

*Hey! Little Hen! When, when, when
Will you lay me an egg for my tea?
Hey! Little Hen! When, when, when
Will you try to supply one for me?*

Hens, like people, were expected to do their best during the war. There were fewer of them in 1939 than there had been five years earlier, but since they could be fed on domestic scraps efforts were made (in vain) to keep their numbers up.

'Supplying an egg' symbolized supplying many other things besides. If people were to be fed during the war – the factory workers (and the children) as much as the armies marching on their stomachs – Britain had to establish a new relationship with nature.

It did so. Total home food production grew by value as a proportion of total consumption between 1939 and 1945. Imports of food, including feeding stuffs, were almost halved. 'Ploughing up' transformed the landscape and agriculture became a controlled industry. Nature looked different too. Every urban allotment – even off Piccadilly – was made to count.

Distributing the food fairly was just as socially important, so it seemed, as producing it. 'Eggs in shell', a technical term, had not made their way at all equally through the kitchens of society before 1939. Recipes might advise two dozen eggs. Some people were lucky to see two a week. During the war, whatever other people's hens achieved by way of production targets, all you could expect on

the ration was thirty at the most, unless you had a priority entitlement. This may have been more than you ever had before. If you kept your own hens of course – or joined a poultry club – you might do better still. Tommy Handley offered his own brand: 'Hello, yolks – have you ever tried ITMA eggs? They're all singing, all humming, and all bumen. The only eggs that are all they're cracked up to be ... With every dozen we give away a gas mask. ITMA eggs can be whipped but they can't be beaten ...'

Rationing was thought of as a *necessary* restriction during the war, and people happily turned the queue into a national institution. Memories of wartime shortages during the First World War were associated with unfair distribution and with profiteering. The Second World War was not to be a war like that. There were black markets – and countryfolk in Cumberland could fare better than town-dwellers in the Midlands – but the Ministry of Food, as much an innovation as the Ministry of Information, was the biggest (and fairest) shop in the world. There were huge penalties for infringing the food regulations, but the absence of a really serious black market is usually said to have been due more to the naturally law-abiding qualities of the British people than to threats of dire consequences. 'It's not clever to get more than your share,' ran the Ministry's warning, and at the end of the war there were women who boasted of never having done so ... Iron rations might have proved incompatible with this high moral line.

"We 'are to take what fish we can get these days, Madam."

people, a different segment, had never tasted corned beef before the war either.) Bread was never rationed until after the war – though wholemeal bread became a favourite propaganda theme (if never a favourite food). The most 'volatile' of all the food rations was cheese. (If you lived in Yorkshire you might be lucky enough to get Wensleydale on the ration.)

The great wartime invention, borrowed from the Germans, was points rationing. This widened choice as much as it could be widened within a rationing system. You could even use your 'natural skill', and choose where to shop without being tied to the grocer where you were registered for basic rations. Not surprisingly, when sweets went on the ration in July 1942, the coupons were called 'personal points'.

'Why should you need a black market, anyway,' one refugee from occupied Europe asked in 1944, 'when you don't even have to ration bread?'

Rationing was first introduced in January 1940, and people were asking for it before it began. For once the government was well prepared and had had ration books ready since 1938. Butter, sugar, bacon and ham were the first goods to go 'on the ration' in January 1940, but things did not get really difficult until 1942. Behind the scenes experts had already concocted a 'Basal Diet' – twelve ounces of bread, a pound of potatoes (precious symbol of national sufficiency), two ounces of oatmeal (Scotland's contribution), an ounce of fat, six ounces of vegetables and six-tenths of a pint of milk a day ... with small supplements, including sugar of course. Fortunately Churchill detested even talking about such diets and the scheme was shelved.

By August 1942 the sugar ration was down to eight ounces and the fats ration down to eight ounces of which only two ounces could be taken in butter. (Some people had never tasted butter before the war.) The meat ration was 1s 2d a week and 2d of this had to go on corned beef. (Some

Of course, some articles off the ration could add an exotic touch to the menu. There was turbot in 1940 and whalemeat in 1942. And there was always rabbit ... Tripe queues formed in Lancashire, while Londoners still rejected it, despite the Radio Doctor's assurance that it was neither 'boiled knitting' nor 'liver struck by lightning'. But even tripe suffered. One of the most pathetic wartime recipes was for 'tripe-and-no-onions'.

As for eggs-in-shell, they were supplemented from 1942 by dried eggs from the United States, 'solid nourishment, easy to ship, cheap to buy'. 'Dried egg is not a substitute at all', as Lord Woolton assured the first unenthusiastic customers. Gradually dried egg became accepted as a staple, and its sudden disappearance in 1945 when Lend Lease ended caused general consternation.

You could do a lot with dried egg if you knew how to do anything at all. And more and more women had to learn. As cooks and kitchen-maids joined the services many better-off women started to cook for the first time. *Vogue* sympathized: 'We know. Your odd man has enlisted. Your second parlour-maid has taken wings towards an RAF canteen. Your kitchen-maid-and-general help has gone to drive a lorry ...' Compromises would have to be made. 'To save your parlour-maid from undue fetch-and-carrying have buffet meals with "help yourself" the general rule ... Serve dishes that are unpretentious, inexpensive, filling and popular. Enormous bowls of spaghetti, noodles, gnocchi or risotto. Thick soup (hare or game soup are always welcome) ...' and, at breakfast, '... cold game pie or chicken galantine as stop-gap'. But this was Christmas 1939 when food was still plentiful, a season when one of the most serious shortages was ground almonds for marzipan. By Christmas 1944 the compromises were greater: Crême Brûlée made of dried egg custard (Ministry of Food recipe) and puddings such as 'Wartime Trifle' which used rum essence and synthetic cream. Over the years the word 'mock' had crept into the cook's vocabulary but she was probably a better cook than she had been in 1939. The era of the *Good Food Guide* and discriminating dining lay

ahead. It had taken a war to teach the British people how to cook and to eat.

It had also taken the Ministry of Food. Presided over in the darkest years by Lord Woolton, the most avuncular of ministers, the Ministry of Food ran its own subsidiary ministry of information complete with spies and scientists. The public had to be guided, cajoled, threatened. The guidance was sometimes witty, the cajolery artful and the threats horrifying. There were Food Facts to read and Food Flashes (soap opera style) to watch in the cinema. But Uncle was at his best in making use of Auntie BBC – through such programmes as the unforgettable five-minute *Kitchen Fronts* after the 8 AM news each day. Even the bureaucracy, which Woolton personalized, prided itself on its own capacity to laugh.

Woolton himself had his own philosophy, that of a highly successful retailer who believed in normal times that today's luxuries should become tomorrow's necessities. He saw rationing as an abnormal wartime phenomenon and was determined to win every battle on the Kitchen Front, including the political one against doctrinaire socialists who wanted to use the war as a means of advancing their political views and perpetuating wartime controls. 'Food control,' he insisted, 'does not mean preventing the other fellow from getting something. It is a means of ensuring that we all get the things that are necessary.'

Some people genuinely changed their food habits during the war. The so-called 'welfare foods' pointed the way to the so-called 'welfare state'. The terrifying malnutrition of the 1930s passed into history. Free orange juice did not make up for the short supply of beer or whisky or even of tea (rationed in July 1940 at two ounces a week per person), but the children liked it better and it did them more good. Milk consumption soared in the poorer families. In some industrial areas milk consumption per head in 1943 had tripled since 1935, despite the fact that in some residential areas it had fallen. Such facts show the powerful effect of the National Milk Scheme and the concentration of limited supplies on 'priority' adults and children.

In general, meals were said to have become much more balanced and adequate during the war. In 1939 half the people in Britain were suffering from some degree of malnutrition and the first wartime Minister of Health (Walter Elliott) had listened to the advice of physiologists in December 1939 that 'a change in the diet of the people was highly desirable'. By 1945 a remarkably similar figure (3000) to that of 1939 for the average daily number of calories consumed per head of the population concealed great changes in distribution. The war *had* brought about fairer shares. Emergency measures had made possible the very reforms which prewar nutritionists had campaigned for in vain.

As in so many other branches of daily life, the war encouraged action outside the home. People had long accused their French neighbours of never eating at home except by grim necessity. Now in Britain itself eating became collective. Works can-

teens suddenly appeared like mushrooms in places where they were genuine 'works wonders'. British Restaurants flaunted national – sometimes local – pride as much as the National Loaf or National Savings. They were to survive the war and in a few cases rationing itself.

Chicken was seldom on the menu although the House of Commons offered *Poulet Ancienne* in 1945. Even for ordinary citizens it was never rationed, merely unobtainable. We needed the hens for the eggs. And the cattle for the milk. Only the pigs were in demand for their own sake – all bacon and pork.

This item in the Women's Institute magazine *Home and Country* in October 1940 speaks for itself . . .

A PIG CLUB AT THE ZOO
A pig club has been started at the zoo. Thirty members of the staff, including a number of keepers, have now added pigs to their charges. The zoo restaurant will be able to make bacon from its saved waste and the pig club has been placed on the boundary of the zoo and Regent's Park where the general public can take an active interest in it.

'Equality in Eating'

(Title of a *New Statesman* article, January 1940)

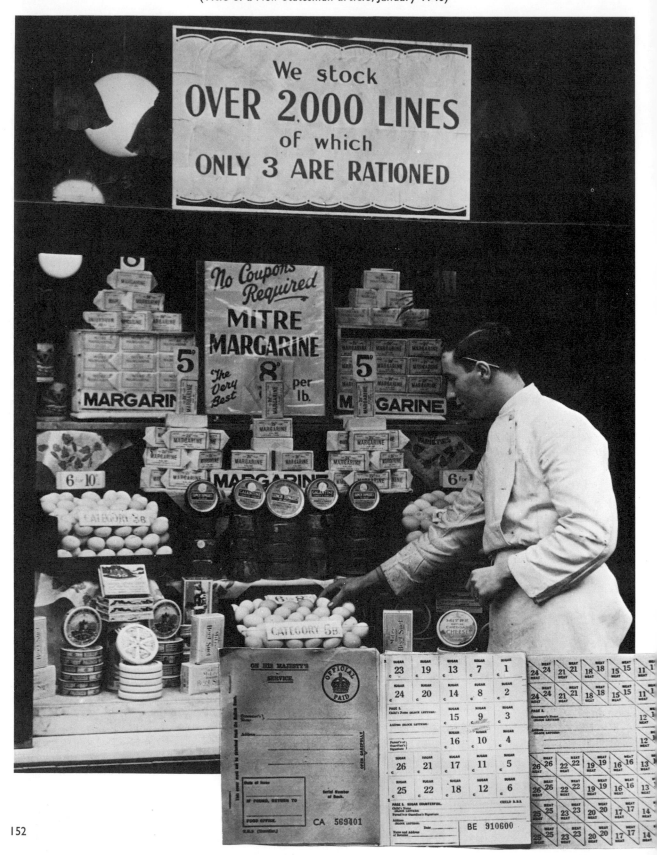

'That dreadful and terrible iniquity . . .'

(*Daily Express* on food rationing, November 1939)

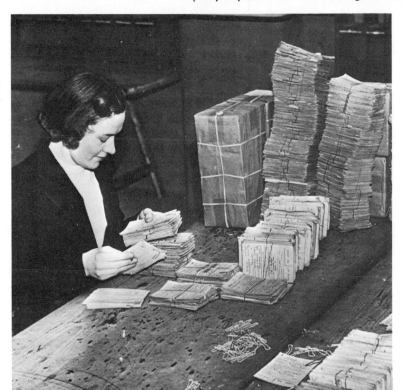

A Gallup Poll on 20 November 1939 showed that six out of ten favoured food rationing. 'It is high time,' wrote Kingsley Martin in the *New Statesman*. 'The ordinary housewife will welcome a measure which offers her the certainty of a regular supply . . . in place of the unlimited uncertainty which has made Friday's shopping a burden in many areas.' The less ordinary citizen accepted rationing too. By February 1940 Molly Panter-Downes reported that it was 'perfectly in order for the weekend guest to arrive with his own little parcel of butter, which he places in the hands of the butler who takes his suitcase'. Only the pressure of the right-wing press (and to some extent of Churchill, then First Lord of the Admiralty) delayed food rationing until January 1940.

(*Left*) A Leeds Food Office employee sorts the new issue of ration books, November 1939.

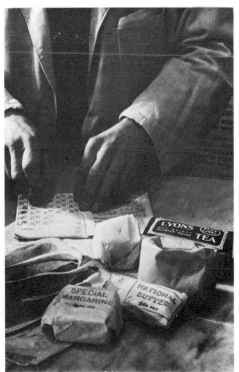

'Fair shares all round'

(Lord Woolton's favourite slogan)

Emergency food offices (painting by Grace Golden, 1941, *below*) were set up during the Blitz for people who had lost their ration books – and even their retailers – and their kitchens. The 'Londoners' Meals Service' set up during the Blitz by the LCC was a more immediate solution to the feeding of hungry homeless people. Its success as an emergency service led to the setting up of British Restaurants as a permanent feature of wartime and even postwar life.

'On points'

Media-conscious Lord Woolton soon got rid of this early Kitchen Front poster (*below centre*) when he became Minister of Food in 1940. 'Let your shopping help our shipping.' 'What could that mean to any ordinary housewife?' he asked. 'She could not repeat it unless she had been very fortunate or very wise in the preservation of her teeth.' Short direct slogans soon took the place of such long-winded efforts: 'Dig for Victory!' 'Don't Waste Bread'. Woolton dropped the preaching; menus replaced morals.

Piles of tins . . . but forbidding 'not for sale' notices in a London store in November 1941 (*left*). Points rationing – a German idea – had been introduced for clothes in June 1941. In November 1941 it was extended to tinned meats, fish and vegetables. From now on it was points rather than money which counted. December 1 was Points Day. Originally planned for 15 November (when this photograph was taken), the Ministry had to postpone it because the shops had not received enough tinned goods. Hence self-denying 'not for sale' signs.

People could distribute their 16 monthly points as they liked, sometimes spending the lot on a delicious tin of salmon, sometimes cautiously stocking up on sensible spam and pilchards.

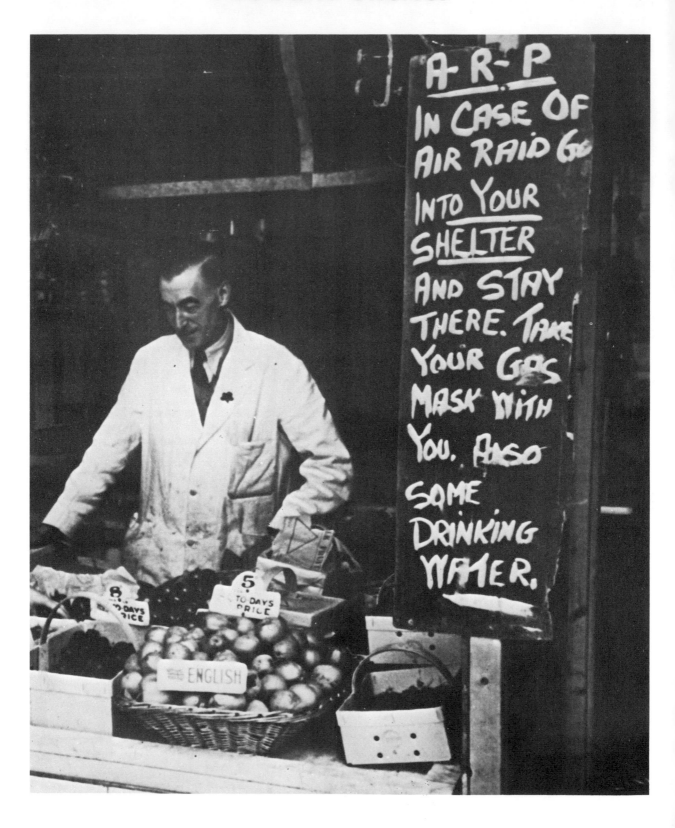

'Lovely Grub'
(The Radio Doctor's favourite expression)

Without Churchill British Restaurants might well have been drearily called 'communal feeding centres'. By 1945 there were 2000 of them serving half a million meals a day. At first they were unpopular with cafe proprietors and restaurateurs, naturally suspicious and jealous of their government aid. Later in the war they were universally accepted. As rationing grew more severe, there was plenty of custom for all eating places from the Ritz to the BR; from Bert's Caff, to the works canteen.

British restaurants could be found anywhere from Sunday Schools (as in Keighley) to the august premises of the Cambridge Pitt Club and the Chinese Department of the Victoria and Albert Museum. Others were newly built. New or old, few had such an appropriate motto as this Borough Restaurant (a local deviant of nomenclature) somewhere in Kent. When J. B. Priestley visited Liverpool's vast new Central Kitchen (also early in 1941) he ate a delicious three course meal for nine pence. Later, in a Postcript Broadcast, he spoke glowingly of 'steaming small holdings' of stew and 'rice pudding by the acre'.

Ploughman's Lunch – only the horse looks doubtful (*below left*). The WVS 'Rural pie scheme' for farm workers in action.

157

How we tightened our belts

A little caviar? And then perhaps a petite Marmite, & shall we say a filet de sole Véronique, with the grape sauce: then what about a Suprême de Volaille or perhaps Poulet à la Maryland with sweet..

Ordering dinner at the Palatial used to be quite a ritual:

Now if you start with that, you can have that after, but not that or any of those: if you begin with this, then you cannot have these, but you could have that or that, or you could choose one of these, unless you wished to have that. Another way would be to cut out that, & go on to that or that, & then you...

Nowadays it is even more so.

NOTICE.

Dishes marked thus ★ or thus ¶ come within the terms of the Food (Restrictions on Meals) in Establishments) Order, 1941, and are restricted.

No person may have more than one dish marked ★ and one marked ¶, or, alternatively, two dishes marked ¶, but other dishes not so marked are unrestricted and may be ordered in addition to, or instead of, restricted dishes.

Déjeuner

VIN en CARAFE
"VIN ROSÉ" (DEMI-SEC)
CARAFE 6/- HALF CARAFE 3/6

VIN en CARAFE
"HOCK"
CARAFE 6/- HALF CARAFE 3/6

HORS D'ŒUVRE

Les Hors d'Œuvre Variés	3/6	Saumon Fumé	5/-
Melon	7/-	Potted Salmon	3/6
Melon Charentais	7/-	Caviar	8/-
Huîtres (½-doz.)	7/-		

SPÉCIALITÉ

Le Lord Woolton Pie 2/6

POTAGES.

Consommé Brunoise à l'Orge Perlé	2/-	Crème Cressonnière	2/-
Consommé Rafraichi, Liquide et en Gelée	2/-		

FARINEUX.

¶ Les Gnocchis de Semoule Portugaise 3/-

LES PLATS DU JOUR

★ La Salade de Homard Savoy	8/-	★ Les Epaules d'Agneau farcies. Sce. Piquante. Velouté Bretonne	7/-
Salad of Lobster.		Stuffed Shoulder of Lamb br'sed. Mashed White Beans. Gherkins Sauce.	
★ Le Maquereau grillée. Sce. Anchois	6/-	★ La Volaille étuvée Bourguignonne	8/-
Grilled Mackerel. Anchovy Sauce.		Surrey Fowl cooked with Red Wine, Onions and Mushrooms.	
★ Le Filet de Haddock Palace	6/-	★ La Fricassée de Volaille glacée Succès	7/-
Fillet of Haddock cooked with Tomatoes and Mushrooms.		Cold Fricassee of Chicken.	
★ Les Tripes à l'Anglaise	5/-	★ La Ravigotte de Poularde Succès	8/-
Tripe with Onions in Cream Sauce.		Salad of Chicken with Julienne of Lettuce and Tomatoes.	
★ Le Chicken Pie en Gelée	8/-	★ Le Grouse Pie rafraichi en Gelée	8/-
Cold Chicken Pie.		Cold Grouse Pie.	
★ La Dinde froide Maison. Salade de Saison	8/-	★ Le Perdreau Rôti (2 couverts)	15/6
Cold Norfolk Turkey.		Roast Partridge.	
★ La Grouse Rôtie (2 couverts) 17/6 (1 couvert)	15/6		
Roast Grouse.			

BUFFET FROID.

★ Langue	4/-	★ Chicken (Wing) 7/- (Leg) 7/-	★ Terrine Maison	5/-	★ Grouse Pie en Gelée 8/-
★ Jambon	4/-	★ Dinde à la Gelée 7/-	★ Galantine	6/-	★ Chicken Pie en Gelée 8/-
			★ Pressed Beef	4/-	

LEGUMES.

Haricots Verts	3/-	Pommes Puree 1/6	Choux Nouveau	2/-	Petits Pois Frais 3/-
Pommes Sautées	2/-	Chouxfleurs Fines Herbes 3/-			Epinards en Purée 2/-
Carottes Nouvelles au Beurre 2/6					

ENTREMETS.

La Poire Condé	4/-	Le Marignan Chantilly 3/-	La Tarte aux Raisins	3/6

GLACES.

		Vanille 3/6 Fraises 3/6	Chocolat 3/6	Le Pouding au Tapioca 2/6

Plats du jour

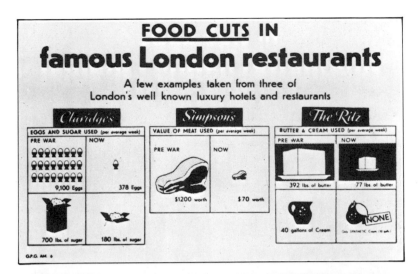

FOOD CUTS IN famous London restaurants

A few examples taken from three of London's well known luxury hotels and restaurants

Claridge's

EGGS AND SUGAR USED (per average week)

PRE WAR	NOW
9,100 Eggs	378 Eggs
700 lbs. of sugar	180 lbs. of sugar

Simpson's

VALUE OF MEAT USED (per average week)

PRE WAR	NOW
$1200 worth	$70 worth

The Ritz

BUTTER & CREAM USED (per average week)

PRE WAR	NOW
392 lbs. of butter	77 lbs. of butter
40 gallons of Cream	Only SYNTHETIC Cream (10 cwt.) NONE

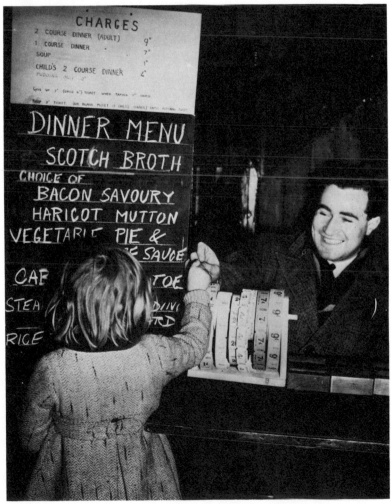

CHARGES
2 COURSE DINNER (ADULT) 9
1 COURSE DINNER 7
SOUP 1
CHILD'S 2 COURSE DINNER 6

DINNER MENU
SCOTCH BROTH
CHOICE OF
BACON SAVOURY
HARICOT MUTTON
VEGETABLE PIE &
SAUCE

Extract from the menu of the Strand Palace, midday 5 February 1943:

Ballotine de jambon Valentinoise
Assiette froide et salade
(Authorized translation by the management)
Hot Spam
Cold Spam

'We not only cope,' the Ministry of Food promised, 'we care.' And so it recommended Woolton Pie (*opposite right* with its namesake), as created by the Chef of the Savoy Hotel . . . and offered on its menu (*opposite below*). Even *The Times* gave the recipe (dignified by the title 'Lord Woolton Pie'): 'Take I lb. each diced of potatoes, cauliflower, swedes and carrots, three or four spring onions, if possible one teaspoonful of vegetable extract and one tablespoonful of oatmeal. Cook all together for 10 mins, with just enough water to cover. Stir occasionally to prevent the mixture from sticking. Allow to cool; put into a pie dish, sprinkle with chopped parsley, and cover with a crust of potatoes or wholemeal pastry. Bake in a moderate oven until the pastry is nicely brown and serve hot with a brown gravy.'

In all restaurants including 'communal feeding centres' (*below left*) meat rations were fixed democratically at one man one pennyworth per meal. The chart (*above left*), published after criticism of lavish hotel and restaurant meals, showed how top London restaurants were hit by restrictions.

In July 1940 it became illegal to serve more than one main course at any restaurant meal. But there was still scope in menu-choosing for the dedicated gourmet (*opposite far left*). In 1942 complaints not of bad menus but of restaurant profiteering led Lord Woolton to introduce the five shilling meal, a flat rate to cover one main course and two subsidiaries, and not to be exceeded by any restaurant from the Ritz downwards.

Cakes and no ale

"*Are you ready to cut the cake, Madam?*"

'There is a simple solution to the cigarette shortage problem. Let women stop smoking. If they gave up the habit their health would be better and tobacco would be available for those for whom Nature intended it.' (Letter in *Daily Telegraph*, 1941)

'Whited sepulchres' (*above right*) were a feature of many wartime weddings after a ban in July 1940 on the making and selling of traditional iced cakes. The tiny cake lurking inside the cardboard or satin superstructure was usually made with dried egg, and gravy browning concealed the absence of dried fruit. The flavouring of rum essence fooled no one. Another *Punch* cartoon shows a bride's mother ordering the couple to 'save the crumbs for the hens and the icing for waste paper salvage'.

The longer the war the thirstier Britain grew. Too many drinkers were chasing too few (often diluted) pints as barley was diverted from breweries to bakeries. One Welsh Minister suggested that the Germans were sparing breweries from bombing because if drinking continued at the present rate we would lose the war.

Barmaid (handing Yorkshire man his pint of beer): 'It looks like rain.'
Yorkshireman: 'Aye, I thought it wasn't beer.'

"OXFORD" MARMALADE

Owing to the requisitioning of our factory at Oxford by the Government we regret that the manufacture of "Oxford" Marmalade must cease until after the War.

October 1942.

FRANK COOPER, Ltd.
OXFORD.

PRODUCED BY THE MINISTRIES OF AGRICULTURE AND INFORMATION

BACON FROM YOUR PIG CLUB
RABBITS FOR EXTRA MEAT
VEGETABLES ALL THE YEAR ROUND
MORE EGGS FROM YOUR HENS

"Off the Ration" Exhibition

ZOO

REGENTS' PARK

AUGUST 3RD TO OCTOBER 3RD · OPEN DAILY FROM 9 A.M.

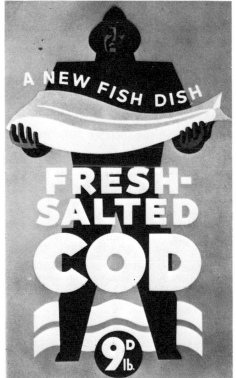

'Off the ration' foods (*above*) like salt cod were publicized as 'grand for children as well as grown-ups and what a bargain! Why not make baked cod with parsnip balls?'

The very best welcome you can give your baby is a beautiful body, a contented disposition — and a healthy, happy mother,

All these depend so much upon your having the right foods and *enough of them.*

As the Radio Doctor says, you have to "eat for one and a bit;" so in addition to your ordinary good mixed diet you need a little extra of certain foods, for the sake of the little one.

So directly you know baby is on the way, get a medical certificate from your doctor, a certified midwife or health visitor. Take or send it with your ration book and identity card to the local Food Office. They will return your book and card together with a green ration book altered to your needs, and the extra clothing coupons.

You are then entitled to

ORANGE JUICE AND VITAMIN A AND D TABLETS

These are not unnecessary fads. They are necessary foods. *The orange juice is rich in vitamin C, which gives vitality and general good health. The tablets which are chocolate coated, are valuable because they contain vitamins A and D, which make for strong bones, good teeth and a sound constitution.*

Jokes about 'Lord Woolton's babies' (and 'preggies') enlivened the official corridors of the Ministry of Food where it was said 'they could get anything out of the Minister if it was for the ladies'. But behind the fun lay solid achievements in what Lord Woolton described as 'preserving the strength of our human stock'.

DOCTOR CARROT guards your Health

The
KITCHEN FRONT

122 WARTIME RECIPES broadcast by Frederick Grisewood, Mabel Constanduros and others, specially selected by the Ministry of Food.

6D. NET

'For all age-groups'

"*I must say I rather like this beige bread!*"

'Doctor Carrot' (*opposite above right*) and 'Clara Carrot' (Walt Disney's own contribution) (*below left*) became substitutes for expensive imports; guardians of health; sources of culinary delight; preservers of schoolgirl complexions; specialized fare to enable you to see in blackouts; secret of the success of ace night-fighter pilots like 'Cats-Eyes Cunningham'. Mixing age-old metaphors of carrots and sticks, patriotic parents gave their children 'carrot stick-jaw', 'deliciously brittle'.

'The Last Resort of a Starving Nation' was *not* the National Wheatmeal Loaf (*above right*), unpopular though it was, but (in the words of W. S. Morrison, Britain's first wartime Minister of Food) the idea of bread-rationing itself, not introduced until 1946.

One means of postponing that evil day was the introduction of the ship-space-saving National Wheatmeal Loaf (*left*). Yet the campaign to popularize it was one of Woolton's few failures. People simply did not like the taste, the look nor the texture of the greyish bread made (after 1942) from flour of 85% extraction . . . despite rumours of its aphrodisiac qualities possibly put out by the Ministry of Food's information section. A few wags even referred to it as 'Hitler's Secret Weapon'.

Britain's non-secret weapon was the Radio Doctor, Charles Hill, 'the doctor with the greatest number of patients in the World'. The eighteen million listeners to his homely *Kitchen Front* broadcasts (*opposite right*) learned what food was good for them, how to cook it . . . and how not to . . . with everything explained, as the *Yorkshire Evening Post* put it, with 'the same unaffected cheerfulness and simplicity and common-sense as Mr Middleton's talks on gardening'.

Eat More Potatoes

(Ministry of Food campaign slogan)

One way to try to save grain was to encourage people to eat more potatoes. The 'Eat-More-Potatoes' campaign was launched in 1940. Potatoes were even used in brewing to save barley. Eating more potatoes proved easier than drinking less whisky. Thanks to Potato Pete and a brilliant team of Ministry of Food publicity experts, potato consumption rose by sixty per cent during the war.

Early in the war the Ministry's language was dignified: 'Potatoes . . . rich store of all-round nourishment', but scarcely dynamic. As the submarine war intensified, so did the war on the Kitchen Front. Potato Pete arrived in 1941 in a blaze of publicity – leaflets, press advertisements and sponsored events, including a scintillating Christmas Potato Fair at John Lewis's bomb site in Oxford Street in 1942 at which each visitor signed a kind of potato pledge: 'I promise as my Christmas gift to sailors who have to bring our bread that I will do all I can to eat home-grown potatoes.'

Jingles such as:

Those who have the will to win
Cook potatoes in their skin
Knowing that the sight of peelings
Deeply hurts Lord Woolton's feelings,

helped and are still remembered. Some of the keener efforts of patriotic cookery journalists might be better forgotten: dismal suggestions on how to extend your margarine for sandwiches 'by melting it and mixing it with mashed potato' or how to stretch your austerity Christmas Cake (already lacking fresh eggs and butter) by substituting grated potato for dried fruit. There were recipes for unpromising dishes called 'Portable Potato Piglets', 'Pigs in Clover' and even 'Inspiration Pie' (runner-up in Lord Woolton's own potato-cookery competition) in which the inspiration lay in using potato for both crust and filling.

POTATOES
feed without fattening and give
you *ENERGY*

"*. . . so I want you all to become even more potato-minded than usual.*"

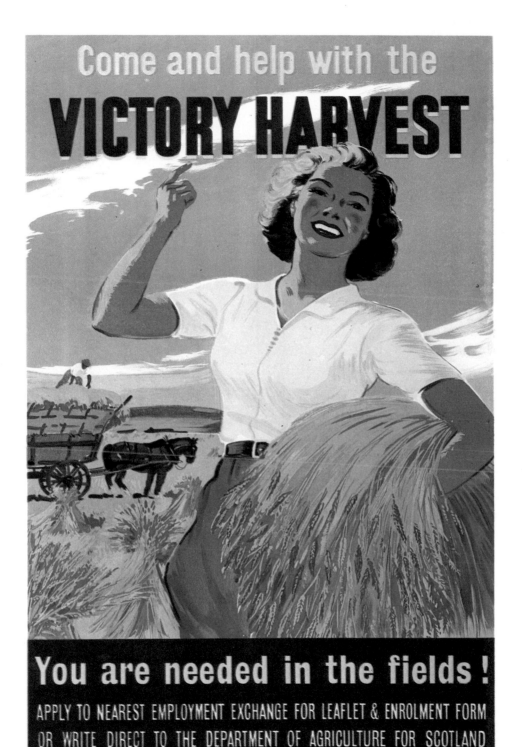

(Overleaf) War Weapons Week in a Country Town by Michael Ford.

Save as you play . . .

Child's cut-out War Savings game.

DIG! DIG! DIG!

Dig ! Dig ! Dig ! And your muscles will grow big,
Keep on pushing in the spade !
Don't mind the worms,
Just ignore their squirms,
And when your back aches laugh with glee
And keep on diggin'
Till we give our foes a wiggin',
Dig ! Dig ! Dig ! to victory.

Lord Haw-Haw used to talk of the English digging their graves. Yet from the earliest months of the war most of the talk of digging in Britain – worms and all – concerned 'digging for victory'. The slogan applied to more than potatoes or carrots: it was used as the title of at least one wartime play – by L. du Garde Peach – and it provided the text for many wartime sermons and wayside pulpits. Backache was a necessary concomitant of the industrial as well as the agricultural war effort. An Oxford University pamphlet referred to 'the sinews of war', the writers of popular songs to muscles, and platform speakers to guts.

It is now clear in retrospect that the British advanced further during the Second World War towards total mobilization of resources than the Germans did, although few people in Britain recognized it at the time. The number of persons registered as unemployed fell from 1,514,000 in 1939 to the incredibly low figure of 75,000 in 1944. And the armaments industry at its 1943 peak (excluding iron and steel) employed over three and a half million people. Priority aircraft production not only registered the most spectacular growth statistics (1938: 2800; 1939: 8000; 1941: 20,000; 1942: 26,000 planes) but made the greatest public impact. You might have to dig for victory in a garden which had lost its iron railings and struggle on the kitchen front in a kitchen where you might have lost your aluminium pots and pans, all to produce more aircraft. You had also been expected to 'save things like paper and cardboard' (the phrase, somewhat surprisingly, was Churchill's own), to avoid waste and go as easy on fuel as on food.

The output of coal was falling in 1940 and 1941 – as the number of miners fell – and in 1942 there was a major fuel crisis. Pits were never as glamorous as aeroplane hangars, but Ernest Bevin, the Minister of Labour, did his best with conscripted 'Bevin boys'. So, too, did the new Ministry of Fuel and Power, set up in June 1942, which needed something more than muscles and spades, let alone slogans like 'Save Fuel for Battle' or advice to restrict bath water to five inches. The proportion of coal cut by machinery increased, as did that of coal conveyed mechanically, but coal output continued to fall, and without open-cast coal the crisis would have continually intensified.

The number of acres under cultivation rose from just under twelve million in 1939 to just under eighteen million in 1945. Digging for victory was more than symbolism. (The admonition 'Lighten our Ships' became as well known as 'Lighten our Darkness'.) By the end of the war Britain imported one third of its food instead of the pre-war two-thirds. Improved agricultural methods were introduced in consequence in a new agricultural revolution. Tractors were deemed as necessary as tanks and between 1938 and 1946 numbers rose nearly four times.

Such statistics were not bandied about during the war as meaningless aggregates: they were converted into popular slogans and driven home in expensive campaigns (those of 1944 cost nearly £2,000,000, including over a quarter by the National Savings Committee). The campaigns appealed not only to immediate self-interest but to everybody's hopes for the future – 'Tanks for Russia' (with real live Russians visiting British factories) as much as 'Tractors for Britain' (with many real live Americans visiting British firms). In the year when Britain stood alone Beaverbrook was the great driving force, demanding 'the impossible' (a word which never figured in his own vocabulary), but it was Ernest Bevin who, unknown to the public, went on to fight a private war with Beaverbrook in 1941, who produced the labour.

Beaverbrook left the Government in February 1942 when Stalin was clamouring for a second front, with the ex-minister's vocal support in the *Daily Express* as vocal as that of any left-wing factory worker. Bevin stayed put throughout the war, 'strong, secure, indispensable'. There were other key figures in the battle for production too, like Leathers who took over War Transport in May 1941 – domestic transport and shipping – and Oliver Lyttelton who replaced Beaverbrook as Minister of Production (the word 'war' was surprisingly dropped). Yet they were relatively little-known and took pains themselves to emphasize how everything in war depended not only on the unknown warriors but on the unknown men and women in the factories.

The women, of course, including the married women, were more photographed than any other section of Britain's wartime population – in corduroy trousers and in factory dungarees just as much as in Auxiliary Territorial Service (ATS), Women's Royal Naval Service (WRNS) or Women's Auxiliary Air Force (WAAF) uniforms. There were 200,000 farm workers in the Women's Land Army in 1944, paid only 28s a week. Less photographed were the women civil servants, forty-eight per cent of the total in a swollen civil service which had expanded from 375,000 to 670,000.

Few would have argued, however, that bureaucracy was winning the war – despite a huge apparatus of control and unprecedented general conscription. The most was made of consensus . . . of work willingly done by 'inner directed' people and of voluntary effort extending what any government could have done. The first official war historians, W. K. Hancock and Margaret Gowing – hard at work even before the war ended – referred to an 'implied contract between government and people', while a wartime White Paper on local government talked not in terms of 'machinery' but of 'a living organism capable of adaptation to new conditions'.

'Blood, toil, tears and sweat' had been promised and they were always demanded from every individual and from every group through to the end. There was even royal backing for what A. J. P. Taylor has called 'war socialism, socialism by consent, that is to say socialism with its difficulties left out'. The King had said in 1940 when the conception of total effort was being forged: 'Each task, each bit of duty, however simple and domestic it may be, is part of our war.' Lady Reading, founder and head of the WVS had made it clear that when it came to. tasks deeds always counted for more than words. 'We have learned', she said at the end of the war, 'that it is no good talking about things, we must do them . . . We have done work we never thought to approach and we have carried burdens heavier than we knew existed.'

Before Churchill became Prime Minister in 1940 the *Manchester Guardian* was asking the Ministry of Information for a government which could 'organise the nation's strength, touch its imagination, command its spirit of self-sacrifice, impose burdens fearlessly on all classes', and by the end of the year – under the country's new management – a leaflet *Victory and Me*, concluding with the King's words, put the leader into language which non-readers of the *Manchester Guardian* could fully understand.

The idea of the 'big national team' – Britain United – comes out most clearly not in speeches but in surviving propaganda and documentary films. Thus George Allison, Arsenal's famous manager, was used in one film, along with the whole Arsenal team, to demonstrate 'what teamwork means in football and in war production'. Thus, also, the government-commissioned film of 1944 *Diary for Timothy*, with a script by someone as unlike Allison as possible, E. M. Forster, was at one with Churchill in message, even in style. 'This was total war. Everyone was in it. War was everywhere. Not only on the battlefields but in the valleys where Goronwy the miner carries his own weapons to his own battlefront.' So, too, did the farmer: as Forster put it, 'The farmer has been fighting against the forces of nature all his life. And now with a mortal enemy upon us he has to fight harder than ever.'

There was a special place for little men in the big team. 'Let Dig for Victory be the motto of everyone with a garden', said the first wartime Minister of Agriculture in 1939 even before the 'big team' had been assembled. The words took wing even earlier than the Spitfires, but the achievement needed no infusions of rhetoric.

Swamps have been reclaimed. Golf courses, sports grounds, city lots, and cemetery extensions are being made to yield food. Famous gardens, once noted for their fragrance, are now given over to cabbages. Britain, in her third year of war, is bringing in the biggest harvest of the century.

Non-farmers do their bit to augment the Nation's food supply. RAF pilots grow radishes beside their machines. Chickens cluck in the fashionable squares of London. A million bees have been turned loose in the heather of Camberley forest. Potatoes are flourishing at Hampton Court and at Sandringham. A field of flax which was planted experimentally by King George V is being extended.

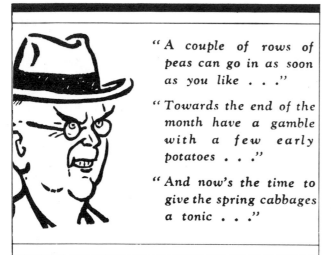

" *A couple of rows of peas can go in as soon as you like . . .*"

" *Towards the end of the month have a gamble with a few early potatoes . . .*"

" *And now's the time to give the spring cabbages a tonic . . .*"

Kensington Gardens, the Hurlingham Polo Club (where a barrage balloon floated over the deserted grandstand) and Hyde Park (with its own piggery) might have been added to the list. But so, too, might countless unnamed places. The number of allotments, the little man's (or woman's) special domain, almost doubled until there were over a million and a half. 'Do not think of your allotment as an ordeal or a war-time sacrifice', wrote the allotment holder's best friend, the famous Mr Middleton, one of the most popular writers and broadcasters of the war, in September 1942. 'Regard it as your pleasant and profitable recreation.' He had his own BBC radio allotment, and tirelessly urged gardeners to 'dig harder to beat the U-boat', to 'Save our Seeds' and to 'turn our gardens into

munition factories, for potatoes, carrots and onions are munitions of war as much as shells and bullets are'. He appealed to beginners 'still undecided whether to dig up the tennis lawn or not' ('don't delay another day') and experts ready to embark on getting sugar from a beetroot ('simple as shelling peas').

There were only a few people who did not respond to the calls of the team manager, particularly when they stuck to agriculture, though they were not lacking their own rhetoric if not logic. A correspondent to the *Glasgow Herald* in 1942 objected to the ploughing up of golf courses on the grounds that it was 'unfair to absent golfers, now in Navy, Army and Air Force, that when they return home they should find their golf courses unplayable, thanks to the folly of those who insisted on their being ploughed up'. A market gardener in Axbridge expressed himself in deeds not words. He objected in April 1941 to substituting cabbages for strawberries, refused to pay a fine and went to gaol.

The factory team was inevitably less easy to manage than the agricultural team. Churchill told war workers that 'the Front Line runs through the factories' and that, in that line, they were 'soldiers with different weapons but with the same courage', while Godfrey Winn, extending the metaphor, talked of the older workers (and the women workers) being able to make up in the factory for what they would not do in the front line. Whatever Churchill or Winn or communist or otherwise, shop stewards might say, there were many deaf ears and some messages of counter-propaganda. Mass Observation noted the views of workers who believed that nothing had really changed in the structures of industry or the basic attitudes of workers towards employers and managers as the war effort intensified. There were even a few, short small and unofficial strikes, a boilermakers' strike in 1944 and several others in the pits (a very different environment from the war factories), echoes of the 'rebellious spirit' evident in sections of the working classes during the 1914–18 war.

That these were, none the less, echoes rather

than intimations of the future was the result of different forces – Labour's participation in the coalition government; trade union support for the war effort; Bevin's position as Minister of Labour. Yet one point stands out. The drastic wartime powers embodied in the Essential Works Order were *not* used (for fear of industrial troubles) and every effort was made in industrial relations as in national and local government to work through consensus. Great efforts were made also to promote 'welfare'. In one propaganda film the canteen manager was displayed as 'a key man'. 'He knows', the film stated explicitly, that 'the industrial army marches on its stomach: the food which passes across the canteen counter is as important to the output of the factory as the steel and aluminium which goes through the workshops . . .'

Films, like *Millions Like Us,* presented an only slightly idealized version of work in a munitions factory, although the personnel were scarcely typical. The workers included Patricia Roc as a sweet simple girl who married an RAF boy from the local camp (they met, of course, at the Works hop), and Anne Crawford as the townee sophisticate ultimately tamed by the honest foreman, Eric Portman. A Ministry of Labour recruiting advertisement showed somewhat less imagination:

When Marion's boy friend was called up, she wanted to be in it too. So she asked the employment exchange about war-work . . . In next to no time they had fixed her up at a Government Training Centre, learning to make munitions . . . And before long she was in an important war job. At last she felt she was really 'doing her bit' . . . Jim was proud of her when he came home on leave. He knows how much equipment counts in modern warfare.

Whatever might be happening to workers' attitudes towards management or the employers – and the number of trade unionists increased from six and a quarter million in 1939 to nearly eight million in 1945 – within the wartime mixed team sex relations generated as much concern as industrial relations.

Old chauvinistic attitudes often died hard. Much of the publicity given to women's war work was due to the fact that such activities *were* still considered extremely unusual, and there was plenty of anti-feminist 'little woman' style mockery as well as old fashioned concern for the weaker sex. Herbert Morrison promised women fire-watchers that they would not have to serve in buildings infested with rats and mice (they were however thought to be capable of coping with an incendiary without shrieks of terror), while James Agate commented in 1943 that 'war or no war, I think the advertisement in the front page of today's *Times* beginning "Lady over Military Age" is ridiculous'. Also in 1943 a nationally-known BBC announcer stated that there was no likelihood of a woman being appointed to his (Mr Alvar Lidell's) job. Pressed to say why, he replied, 'She might have to read bad news.'

Working men's attitudes were different without being any less chauvinistic. 'Many times I have heard other men say,' one man remarked cautiously in 1942, "I wish to hell my old woman wasn't above the age limit".'

Even the Public Relations Officer to the Ministry of Supply, who had little to say about crèches, stated that 'cosmetics are as essential to a woman as a reasonable supply of tobacco is to a man', and the Royal Ordnance Factory issued an attractive booklet, *ROF Beauty Hints: Look to your Looks,* whilst a welfare officer at a munitions factory believed that '£1000 worth of cosmetics, distributed among my girls, would please them more than £1000 in cash.' (Bless their silly little heads!) *Vogue*, too, remained dedicated to the ideal of the feminine woman whose primary role was 'to maintain the good spirits of the fighting man . . .'

And what do hers depend on? Well, largely on her looks. This business of looking beautiful is definitely a duty. When you look your best, you feel self confident and your confidence transmits itself to those around you.

True to this policy, and said to be one of the sights of London, were the volunteer ambulance drivers (female) taking their driving tests in Hyde Park 'careering madly on and off the bridle paths swathed in silver fox and rattling with pearls'.

Working men were not taken in by such frivolity. Many of them believed like the Nazis that women's place was the home and feared that the admission of women to traditionally male-held jobs might cause unemployment in a world which, after the war, might not provide enough jobs for both men and women. This comment (from a Mass Observation Report of 1942) by a north-country factory manager shows this attitude.

This girl has so taken to machinery that she'd like to become an apprentice and go right through the works. This of course is not possible on account of Union agreements. There's a feeling among the men at the moment women must be in the factory solely because of the war but really women's place is the home . . .

Even the home, however, was thought of as part of the front line and the fire in the hearth as a kind of furnace. Housework was dignified as war work, and the housewife was told to remember that hers was 'a wartime job too'.

'I try to do it even better than usual', said the government's model housewife. 'I shop with a special care. I waste nothing. I save paper, tin, bones . . . I try to keep myself and my house trim and cheerful. I take special pains with the cooking because I know this keeps the men's spirits up. I send the children to bed early and I don't stay up listening for sirens. I remind myself in this way, though I may not be winning medals, I am certainly helping to win the war!'

A government propaganda film, They Also Serve, addressed the Housewives of Britain as 'the Force behind the Fighting Line'.

All kinds of unmilitary and unproductive activities were praised as war-work, from make-do-and-mend ('a neatly patched garment is something to be proud of') to keeping pigs and chickens. In 1940 foster-mothers of evacuees got a letter from the Queen herself, in which she wrote praising 'the service you have rendered to your country in 1939 . . . By your readiness to serve you have helped the State in a work of great value.' If, on the other hand, you were the mother of an evacuee who had obediently left her child in the 'safe' area the Government praised your restraint as valuable service in 'preserving the nation's stock'.

Cottage, however humble, and mansion both had their appointed place. Owners of country houses lent their homes for the war effort, turning them into hospitals which they sometimes, with varying degrees of success and friction, ran themselves.

It was never easy to separate out facts and images in relation to the war effort. Perhaps the most famous munitions factory of all was located not in Coventry, Birmingham or Belfast, but at Foaming at the Mouth, where Tommy Handley by 1942 was both local mayor and Factory Manager. It was never clear what the factory was making, but the jargon was said to have been collected from a trip through the Wellington Bomber works at Chester by the writer and producer. Funf threatened: 'This is Funf speaking. Your factory will never open.' Tommy Handley, 'We make everything from wardens' posts to whoopee . . . Here is a typical shift arriving punctually from eight to ten AM or thereabouts.' And the song,

We're so happy to be working in the ITMA factoree.
You won't find us idly lurking
In a place we shouldn't be.

Yet, whatever the images, the hard facts were indisputable. The war did mean a change in habits and in styles. As one of the near-surrealist conversion tables issued by the Board of Trade put it:

IN WARTIME, production must be for war and not for peace. Here are examples of the changeover from peacetime products to wartime necessities:
CORSETS become Parachutes and Chinstraps
LACE CURTAINS become Sand-fly Netting
CARPETS become Webbing Equipment
TOILET PREPARATIONS become Anti-Gas Ointments
GOLF BALLS become Gas Masks
MATTRESSES become Life Jackets
SAUCEPANS become Steel Helmets
COMBS become Eyeshields

ISSUED BY THE BOARD OF TRADE
You may wish to cut out this page and display it to your customers

It was not surprising in such circumstances that fashion could become utility, or most daringly of all that women (in defined circumstances) might almost become men.

SAVE WASTE PAPER!
Every Scrap Shortens the Scrap!

BILLY PLONKIT: *"I've turned in all our band-parts to the Waste Paper Campaign, fellers, and written out our special choruses on the backs of envelopes. After all, it ain't what you do—it's the way that you do it!"*

Utility furniture expressed the spirit of the times as much as utility clothes (which still tolerated wide men's trousers while discountenancing long women's skirts). Indeed furniture provided, at the time and in retrospect, an example of total state control over the supply of a scarce material, timber, over designs (January 1941 saw the first 'Standard Emergency Furniture') and price (through standardization). The CC41 utility sign became one of the best-known of all wartime symbols. Of course, it was best of all if you did not need to buy, if you made-do and mended . . . and if you saved every piece of scrap ('every scrap helps the Scrap') in order 'to salvage the raw materials of victory' (another of Churchill's phrases).

The rubbish heap was, in its way, made to seem as important as the factory. Beaverbrook told his fellow countrymen in 1942 that if they could turn in a hundred thousand tons of waste paper he could divert twenty-five thousand tons of shipping to the transporting of war supplies to Russia. A Wiltshire lady, quoted in the *New Statesman's*

'This England' (a weekly column which collected absurd sayings), asked whether it would not be wise 'to make use of the thousands, or hundreds of thousands of books stored in the British Museum'. Could they not 'serve the country'? Whilst a Dunfermline Town Councillor declared in 1942, 'There are only two books worth keeping in any house – your Bible and your bankbook.' The editor of *Everywoman* was less philistine, although just as vehement:

Every woman [she argued] who destroys a scrap of precious paper destroys the means of making British weapons just as surely as if she helped to blow up a munitions dump! Every woman who keeps a store of paper in her home, old bills, letters, unread books, finished periodicals, wrapping paper, cardboard boxes, is automatically forcing a ship to make a perilous journey on the high seas to fetch that quantity of paper carelessly ignored by her.

Even blitzed buildings were made to yield their quotas of salvaged materials. The RAF used large quantities of rubble for runways and part of the rest was used as ballast for ships sailing to America. Some of it is said – or at least Americans were told that it was – to have been used to make road surfaces in New York City.

Diversion of materials from consumers to the nation and from waste to weapons of war was not the only diversionary theme of the war effort. Bevin, like the social psychologists, believed in music while you work. The output of radio valves increased from under twelve million a year to over thirty-five million in 1944, and although few of those made their way to BBC Home Service Listeners, the BBC flourished in wartime through its role as a medium of entertainment as much as through its role as a channel of guidance. In *Music While You Work*, the BBC's *Handbook for 1942* stated, John Watt and his colleagues, supplying 'the machinery of entertainment', 'succeeded in combining work and play to the acknowledged improvement of the former'. And you did not always need professionals. *Works Wonders* with its reliance on untested local talent could often do the trick.

Dig for Victory

Prince Albert would have approved . . . Early peas climbing up twigs on the allotments near the Albert Memorial, 1942.

DIG FOR VICTORY

'Plough Now'

GROW FOOD FOR THE NATION
FEEDING STUFFS FOR YOUR FARMS
KEEP OUR SHIPS AND MONEY FREE
FOR BUYING VITAL ARMS

'Every endeavour must be made . . . to grow the greatest volume of food of which this fertile island is capable.' (Churchill, November 1940)

The Minister of Agriculture exhorted not only 'the big man with the plough' but the 'little man with the spade', whilst *Vogue* advised its hitherto leisured readers to get digging: 'Our land, whether inherited acres or a council allotment, now has but one significance – FOOD. It is the nation's larder . . . Now is the time to plough up the park [presumably one's own] and make over the flower beds for vegetables . . .' 'Last year gardeners timed their prize blooms for the coming out party of the daughter of the house. This year they time prize vegetables for the coming on leave of the son of the house.'

'Backs to the Land'

(Bawdy version of Women's Land Army motto)

Back to the land, we must all lend a hand.
To the farms and the fields we must go.
There's a job to be done,
Though we can't fire a gun
We can still do our bit with the hoe.
When your muscles are strong
You will soon get along
And you'll think that country life's grand;
We're all needed now,
We must all speed the plough
So come with us – Back to the Land.
(The Land Army Song)

'My two land girls wanted to bath before the kitchen fire, and I had to wait outside in the snow. One, a London actress, shouted through the keyhole, "Come in and dry my back." That is not the type of girl wanted.'
(Farmer quoted in *Sunday Express*)

"Now, Miss Fforbes-Wattson, have you had any experience of agricultural work?"

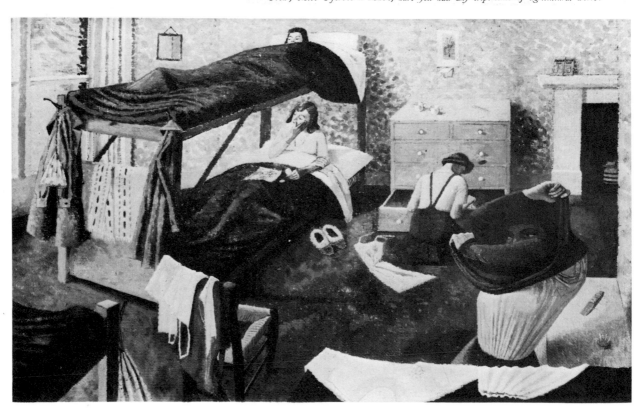

'And where do they go from here?'

(Title of a *Vogue* article, 1945, on the future of women after the war)

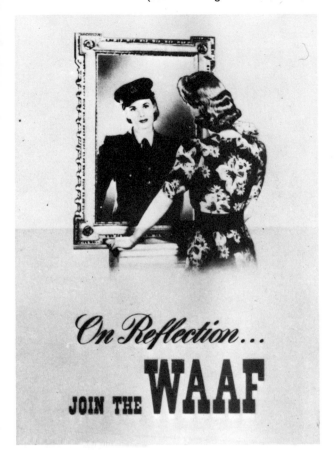

On Reflection . . .

JOIN THE **WAAF**

'British women officers often give orders to men. The men obey smartly and know it is no shame. For British women have proved themselves in this war. They have stuck to their posts near burning ammunition dumps, delivered messages afoot after their motor-cycles have been blasted from under them. They have pulled aviators from burning planes . . . There isn't a single record of any British woman in uniformed service quitting her post, or failing in her duty under fire. When you see a girl in uniform with a bit of ribbon on her tunic, remember she didn't get it for knitting more socks than anyone else in Ipswich.' (From the US War Department booklet for GIs entering Britain in wartime, 1942)

(*Left*) Jokes like 'Up with the lark and to bed with a Wren' did not apply to these officers.

'Hit back with National Savings'

(Government slogan)

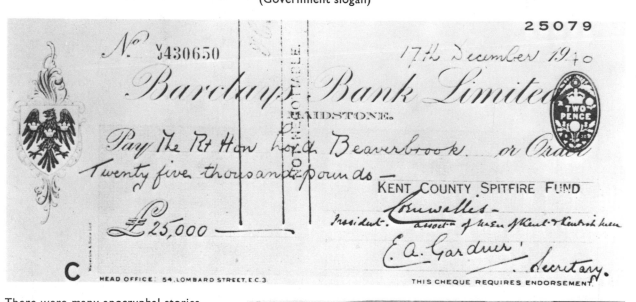

There were many apocryphal stories illustrating Lord Beaverbrook's energy: 'Lord Beaverbrook (then Minister of Aircraft Production) telephones an aircraft factory and tells the manager that he must have another bomber ready a week ahead of schedule. "I'm afraid, Lord Beaverbrook, that will be impossible." "Impossible," roars Lord B, "is a word not included in my vocabulary. I shall be at the factory on the date I mentioned." Came the day, came Lord B. On the tarmac stood a bomber. Around it bobbed the manager. "Well," demanded Lord B., "is she ready?" "Well, my Lord," began the manager nervously. "Splendid," says Lord B. "She is to fly to Berlin at once. Here are the pilot and crew." In they got and off they took. They reached Berlin. They found their target. The bomber got the signal, pulled the lever – and out tumbled the entire night shift of the factory.'

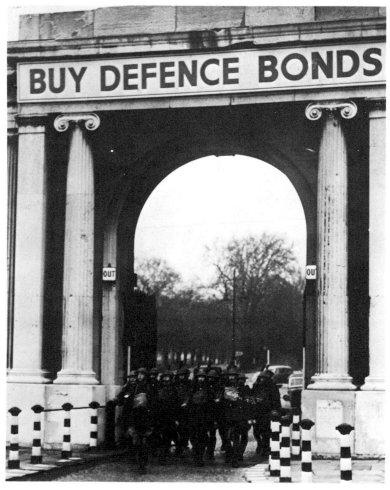

'Lend, Don't Spend'

(Government slogan)

The real economic importance of the savings campaigns lay in the anti-inflationary effect of diverting private spending, but the popular campaigns of the war – War Weapons (1941), Warships (1942), Wings for Victory (1943), and Salute the Soldier (1944) as well as Beaverbrook's original Spitfire Funds of 1940 (*opposite above*) – encouraged donors to believe that their money was buying specific items – from the City of Leeds (100 four-engined bombers and 200 fighters in Wings for Victory week) to a schoolboy who sent a guinea for a Spitfire's thermometer.

School for Savings

14th Oct

How I Can Help.

I can help win the war by having ~~moor~~ national ~~Naional~~ Sav-ing Stamps, ~~you~~ the can buy at School, the money goes to the Government, and pays for the stuff to make guns

aeroplanes, ships and tanks.

Another way in which I can help win the war is by going without sweets, for the Government need the stuff for other things.

Yet another way in which I can help to win the war is by picking up potatoes and let the other people do other things such as ~~d~~ haymaking.   National Government

21st Oct

Composition

on

Trafalgar Day

To-day I ~~are~~ am going to tell you about what happened on The 21 st of Oct. which is when Napoleon

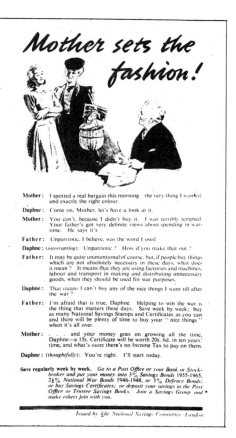

Mother sets the fashion!

Mother : I spotted a real bargain this morning — the very thing I wanted and exactly the right colour.

Daphne : Come on, Mother, let's have a look at it.

Mother : You can't, because I didn't buy it. I was terribly tempted. Your father's got very definite views about spending in war-time. He says it's

Father : Unpatriotic, I believe, was the word I used.

Daphne : (interrupting): Unpatriotic ? How d'you make that out ?

Father : It may be quite unintentional of course, but, if people buy things which are not absolutely necessary in these days, what does it mean ? It means that they are using factories and machines, labour and transport in making and distributing unnecessary goods, when they should be used for war purposes.

Daphne : That means I can't buy any of the nice things I want till after the war ?

Father : I'm afraid that is true, Daphne. Helping to win the war is the thing that matters these days. Save week by week ; buy as many National Savings Stamps and Certificates as you can and there will be plenty of time to buy your " nice things " when it's all over.

Mother : . . . . and your money goes on growing all the time, Daphne—a 15s. Certificate will be worth 20s. 6d. in ten years' time, and what's more there's no Income Tax to pay on them.

Daphne : (thoughtfully): You're right. I'll start today.

Save regularly week by week. Go to a Post Office or your Bank or Stock-broker and put your money into 3% Savings Bonds 1955-1965, 2½% National War Bonds 1946-1948, or 3% Defence Bonds; or buy Savings Certificates; or deposit your savings in the Post Office or Trustee Savings Banks. Join a Savings Group and make others join with you.

Issued by the National Savings Committee, London

The Squander Bug campaign was a different approach to saving . . . and more honest: it was simply not spending that was important. Even schoolchildren were effectively indoctrinated (see extract [left] from a school composition by the author, aged eight, 1941).

'Various sums have been raised for the war and other charities.' (From a Women's Institute Report, August 1942)

'Ask the WVS'

'Saucepans into Spitfires'

'Women of Britain, give us your aluminium. We want it and we want it now . . . We will turn your pots and pans into Spitfires and Hurricanes, Blenheims and Wellingtons . . .' (Lord Beaverbrook, July 1940)

Woman to friend as they watch Spitfires overhead: 'I suppose after the war they'll melt them down and make saucepans and things.' (*Punch*, 1941)

Comment overheard during salvage of railings (*below*): 'We didn't shout when our sons were requisitioned, so why make a fuss about this?' Others referred to the class barriers which were also being removed . . .

'Though park railings in Manchester are being removed for scrap, the park gates will be retained and locked as usual at night to indicate that the parks are in theory closed.' (*Manchester Daily Dispatch*, July 1940)

'One envelope makes 50 cartridge shells'

(From a Government salvage chart, 1942)

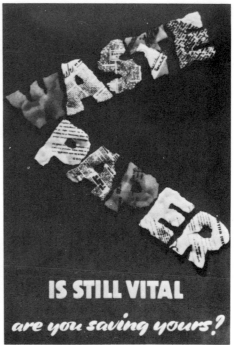

IS STILL VITAL

are you saving yours?

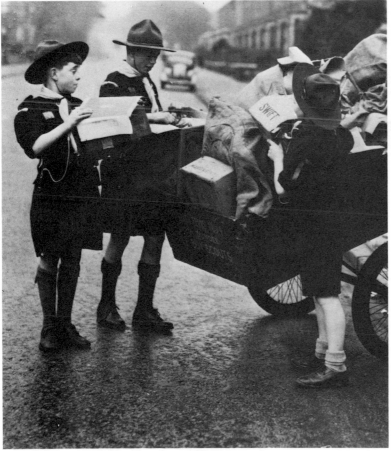

The war is driving Hitler back
But here's one way to win it:
Just give your salvage men the sack
And see there's plenty in it.
(Government jingle)

One old lady bringing in salvage was worried about her love letters. 'If I bring in a lot of old letters will anyone read them?' she asked. The salvage collector assured her that the letters would not be read, but suggested that she could tear them into small pieces. 'Perhaps I will,' said the old lady, 'but if I can't part with them, I'll bring a lovely set of false teeth instead.'

Another old lady, Queen Mary, was also a formidable salvage collector. In 1943 Godfrey Winn reported enthusiastically, 'Queen Mary never uses a new envelope and on the course of her drives to visit camps and aerodromes and factories, wherever she sees salvage lying around unclaimed – bones, bottles, scrap iron – Her Majesty stops the car, has it picked up, and taken home in triumph to the village dump.'

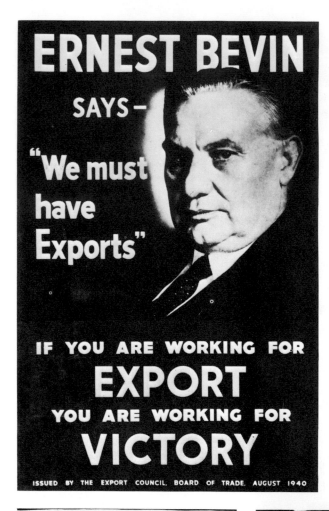

ERNEST BEVIN
SAYS –
"We must have Exports"

IF YOU ARE WORKING FOR
EXPORT
YOU ARE WORKING FOR
VICTORY

ISSUED BY THE EXPORT COUNCIL, BOARD OF TRADE, AUGUST 1940

WOMEN OF BRITAIN
COME INTO
THE FACTORIES

ASK AT ANY EMPLOYMENT EXCHANGE FOR ADVICE AND FULL DETAILS

Gad, sir, Lord Sportingsquirt is right.
It's only fair we should give the Germans
a good start this war. After all, we
won last time, y'know.

RETURN MATCH by BLIMP

Goodnight – and Go To It!' (Herbert Morrison, broadcast 1941)

'They never want us in Sheffield until there's a war.' (The Master Cutler, quoted by J. L. Hodson, April 1940)

'We have come through the collapse of other countries and bombardment of our own, and we have proved to ourselves that we can take it. So we are not worrying about that anymore. We are now at the beginning of a period of giving it.' (Tom Harrisson in a broadcast to North America, July 1941)

'He forgets his lunch in the description by a fighter pilot of the performance of *his* plane over Germany. Ned Sparks is an acetylene welder in a Halifax assembly shop.' (Contemporary [1942] caption to photograph *above left*)

Factories made everything – including thingumebobs:
She's the girl that makes the thing that drills the hole that holds the spring That drives the rod that turns the knob that works the thingumebob.

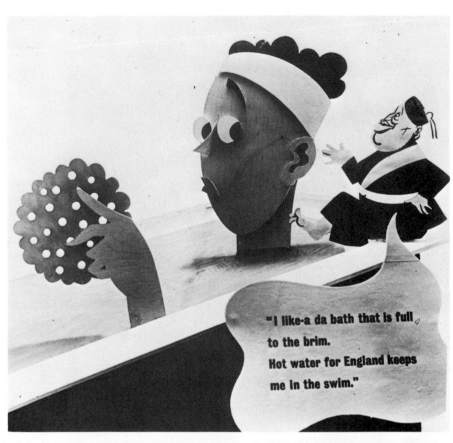

"I like-a da bath that is full
to the brim.
Hot water for England keeps
me in the swim."

. and Power

Ernest Bevin spent as much time explaining how important it was to dig for coal as other ministers explained that it was to dig for victory. The Bevin boys (even when they were Old Harrovians, chosen by ballot) were never quite as glamorous as even the Land Army girls. The BBC certainly did its best with Fuel Flashes, and posters extolled coal substitutes (*opposite above left*) and (indirectly) small tepid baths (*opposite above right*). Henry Moore (*opposite below*) did not need the assistance of Mussolini's bath-tub image and caught the spirit of industrial revolution drawings.

Many miners remained revolutionary and sometimes went on strike (*left* a 1944 Welsh coal strike at Mountain Ash) despite the exhortations of the newly-founded Ministry of Fuel and Power and their own trade-union leaders. Most miners worked hard in depressing conditions. Mountain Ash removed its Union Jack during its strike, the flag which had flown earlier to celebrate its record output. Most miners were dreaming not of home but of post-war nationalization . . . even on Sunday mornings down the pits (*below*). Yet less coal was being dug with more machinery (and older men – most of the Bevin Boys were employed on haulage and maintenance only) in 1945 than in 1939.

NOTICE

IT HAS BEEN DECIDED TO WORK ON SUNDAY MORNING FEB. 16TH AS A FULL COAL SHIFT. EVERY MAN IS EXPECTED TO WORK ON SUNDAY AND THROUGH THE WEEK TO HELP IN THE NATIONAL EMERGENCY.
EVERY MAN IS EXPECTED TO PULL HIS WEIGHT

Think of the Wounded!

GIVE ALL YOU CAN TO THE

RED CROSS & ST. JOHN

WARSHIP WEEK

A message from the PRIME MINISTER

10, Downing Street. Whitehall.

I wish all success to the National Savings Movement in the Warship Weeks Campaign. The results will, without doubt, provide still further proof of our determination to press home this fight until victory is won.

The campaign deserves the support of all who desire to see, as I do, still closer links forged between our towns and villages and the Royal Navy, which unceasingly protects and keeps open for all freedom-loving peoples the Highways of the Seas.

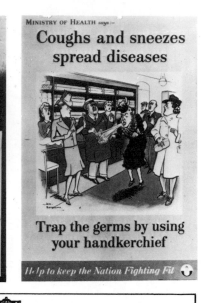

MINISTRY OF HEALTH says:—

Coughs and sneezes spread diseases

Trap the germs by using your handkerchief

Help to keep the Nation Fighting Fit

"Can I persuade you to increase your penny a week from twopence to threepence?"

WANTED

125,000

BINOCULARS FROM THE PUBLIC

OUR FIGHTING SERVICES NEED THEM ALL!

SELL YOURS NOW!

The Services must have every good pair of binoculars they can get. They want them at once.

Binoculars take a long time to make. The highly-skilled labour necessary is working night and day on gun-sights and other vital war instruments; so the Ministry of Supply asks all private owners of binoculars to offer them to the Government.

In every town opticians are acting as authorised collecting agents—giving their services free. They will display Ministry of Supply posters.

If you possibly can, take your binoculars to the nearest optician; you will be given an official receipt. Or you can send them, registered post, to the Ministry of Supply, 191 Regent Street, London. Tie on a label with your name and address and endorsed "Sale" or "Gift".

It is known that there are 125,000 suitable binoculars in Great Britain—every pair is needed! Put your pair on active service—they are wanted

URGENTLY

ISSUED BY THE MINISTRY OF SUPPLY

YOUR MOBILE CANTEEN IN ACTION

Your Mobile Canteen is filled with food and hot drinks and all the incidentals that the soldier or airman can want. It starts out on its journey.

The canteen calls at many isolated posts: balloon barrage units and anti-aircraft gun sites. The arrival of the canteen is a bright spot in the men's day.

The men on duty in these lonely places take a few minutes off to drink hot tea or smoke a cigarette and hear the news. Often this is the only contact they have with the outside world during the long, lonely weeks between leave periods.

Thank you, Dominica!

Other war gifts from Dominica include subscriptions to the Fund for the Red Cross and St. John War Organisation, Aid to China, Navy Comforts Fund, Anti-Aircraft Command Welfare, St. Dunstan's, R.A.F. Comforts, Merchant Navy Comforts, King George's Fund for Sailors, and the Shipwrecked Fishermen and Mariners' Benevolent Society.

Slogans like 'Go To It' were no use to mothers of small children without day nurseries (*below right* pram-pushing mothers follow a recruiting van to make the point). Other married women war-workers found it impossible to combine shopping for the family with long hours of work. A propaganda film (1941) showed a smiling housewife showing her government priority shopping card to her equally smiling grocer ('Her things are ready for her. No queueing. No waste of time . . . One of the ways of solving the problems of the Home Front . . . the people on the spot getting together. Seeing what has to be done and then doing it'). (*Below*) A lady Underground cleaner poses and (*right*) Queen's messengers get on with the job of providing food and first aid to bomb victims.

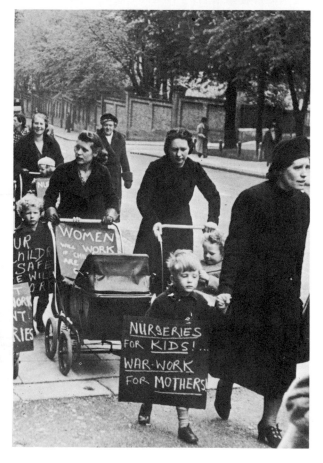

. . and we cannot have it both ways'

(From an advertisement for Yardley cosmetics, July 1942)

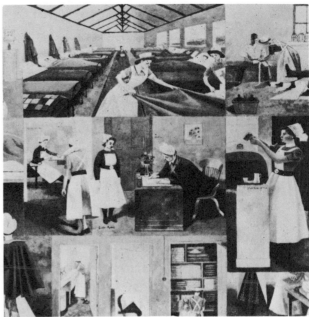

"A first-class workman's ticket to Hayford, please."

I'm only a wartime working girl,
The machine shop makes me deaf,
I have no prospects after the war
And my young man is in the RAF
    K for Kitty calling P for Prue . . .
    Bomb Doors Open . . .
    Over to You.

Night after night as he passes by
I wonder what he's gone to bomb
And I fancy in the jabber of the mad
  machines
That I hear him talking on the intercom.
    K for Kitty calling P for Prue . . .
    Bomb Doors Open . . .
    Over to You.

(From 'Swing-Song' by Louis MacNeice)

(Above) St Thomas's Hospital carried on in evacuated premises (painting by Evelyn Dunbar).

'Please do not hesitate to take such lead as is demanded of you . . . WVS is looked upon as a strong, efficient machine which can carry an immense load.' (Lady Reading, WVS Chairman, 1940). One Dundee member (above left) took the advice literally . . .

'Our Gracie delivers the goods'

(From the film *Stage Door Canteen*, 1944)

Let us on to the task, to the toil!
Guard the streets, heap the arms, lead the
brave . . .

Build the ships, rule the sky, lend to save,
Wish me luck as you wave me goodbye.
(Sagittarius, *New Statesman*, February 1940)

BE LIKE THE KETTLE AND SING

When your troubles are boiling over
Consult this recipe
Everybody can be in clover
Happy as can be . . .
When you're up to your neck in hot water
Be like the kettle and sing.

Wartime entertainment was not just one long succession of *Works Wonders*, the kind of entertainment which thrived on direct participation, or a protracted *Workers' Playtime* 'sustaining morale' and giving workers everywhere 'a sense of kinship'. The 'recipe' for entertainment, as the 1943 song put it, was more complicated than the words of the song itself suggested. Five and a half million people might listen to *Music While You Work* but the BBC had a different recipe for every day of the week beginning with *Monday Night at Eight* and including a Wednesday symphony concert (from the BBC's evacuation centre in Bedford), and *In Town Tonight* on Saturdays – it enjoyed its 250th performance in June 1941 – and the Sunday night *Epilogue*.

The presence of the last of these items on the weekly list is a reminder that there was more praying as well as more singing in wartime. There was also more serious music as well as *Music While You Work* (blessed by the Industrial Welfare Society). 'When I feel tired and full of doubts,' said the actor Robert Donat in 1940, 'I turn to the unfailing solace and courage of music, especially the music of Bach's Chorale Prelude "Sanctify us by Thy Goodness".' Lastly, there was more talking, too – arranged not only by the prestigious Talks Department of the BBC but by the Ministry of Information itself. *The Brains Trust* (which started with the title of *Any Questions* in January 1941) attracted 29·4 per cent of the total listening audience, a staggering figure, for the series of 1944–5; and for every BBC Brains Trust in the studio there were a score in the country. As *Truth* put it in 1944, 'from Joad, Hogg and Co. down to the Little Piddlington Allotment Brains Trust, there is infinite variety'.

The BBC was in a very special position in the world of entertainment during the war. For a time – at the very beginning – it had a near monopoly – with only the public houses to challenge it. 'All cinemas, dance halls and places of public entertainment will be closed until further notice', the Home Office announced, adding for good measure, 'Football matches and outdoor meetings of all kinds which bring large numbers together are prohibited until further notice.' 'If the public houses are not subject to the same curfew,' remarked *Melody Maker*, not usually associated with Temperance views, 'we may expect an alarming increase in alcoholism.' There was little to do in fact except drink in September 1939 or listen to the BBC's single Home Service programme (television, reserved for the London area had shut down already, with a Mickey Mouse cartoon). The *Sunday Pictorial*, which along with everybody else did not like the single programme, felt that this was the first 'scandal' of the war, and Arthur Greenwood, who is said to have spoken for Britain when he had urged the need for Britain to stand firm against Hitler only a few weeks earlier, was still speaking for Britain when he attacked the BBC's 'Weeping Will' attitudes.

Unfortunately the BBC was not allowed to explain why it was offering such a restricted service – Chamberlain, indeed, had believed at one stage before the war that it too should be shut down – but it very soon got over the agonies of the first twelve weeks. There was never any shortage of controls, but between the month of February 1940, when it introduced an alternative service, and VE-Day in 1945, it provided more or less what listeners needed or perhaps even wanted. The second programme was called the Forces Programme although the Forces were always in a minority among the listeners, and it was free from some of the old, therefore self-imposed, BBC restraints, notably the Sunday policy. The range of both the Forces and the Home Service Programmes was very wide, however (important when newspapers were cut so drastically in size); stirring war commentaries (particularly after the tides of battle had turned), inspiring postscripts (J. B.

Priestley rivalled Churchill); and imaginative 'features' (hailed rightly as expressions of the 'Art of Radio'), through to *Garrison Theatre*, *Happidrome* and ITMA, along with music for every taste, and morning and evening prayers, which in October 1940 had audiences respectively of nearly three million and nearly one million and a quarter. This was a religious war, said Dr Garbett, the Archbishop of York, 'like the wars of the sixteenth and seventeenth centuries'.

The re-opening of Sunday amusements shocked more than clergymen, although the Rector of Edgware Parish Church was more shocked than most when he told his parishioners in October 1939 that 'an act of reverence towards God shown by closing such places on His day would draw down His blessing, which may be forfeit if we act so carelessly'.

The shocking never stopped, but neither did the Windmill, which boasted that it never closed and became a symbol of Britain 'carrying on'. Some famous city theatre companies, like the Birmingham Rep, had chequered histories of closing, opening, closing and opening, but there was more appreciation of the 'living theatre' in all its forms than there had been during the 1930s. The forms varied. Thus, after the arrival of the Americans *Stage Door Canteen* was a great success as was *This is the Army*, attended by the King and Queen and the two princesses, even though it included a strip-tease act by Gipsy Rose Lee.

Art seemed to count for more in war than it had done in peace. In October 1939 Clive Bell, in a *New Statesman* article, pleaded for a Ministry of Arts, and after the war Britain was to get, if not a Ministry, at least an Arts Council (with J. M. Keynes struggling to settle both the economic and the aesthetic future of the country). 'It would be a poor thing,' Bell wrote, 'if in the process of resisting barbarism we lost our own civility.' Bloomsbury's contribution to the Second World War (lampooned in the *Daily Express*) was more striking than its contribution to the First, for only a month later Kenneth Lindsay, the Parliamentary Secretary to the Board of Education, not only

paid his proper respects to Sir Kenneth Clark, but talked of Government 'initiative' in the arts. The pictures had been moved out of the National Gallery but the wartime concerts had already started, and in January 1940 the Government did its bit, too, when it set up the Council for Education in Music and the Arts, CEMA, not quite as familiar initials as NAAFI (Navy Army and Air Force Institutes), and ENSA (for Forces only), but nearly. A grant of £25,000 was worth quite a lot of eloquent articles and speeches . . . though not as much as NAAFI/ENSA's income which rose from just under £500,000 in the first year of the war to nearly £2 million in the third.

With CEMA's encouragement of 'British Cultural Services' (the dry word 'services' ensured the right appeal) and the interests of 'culture workers' (ditto), it was possible for the arts to spread beyond London to the provinces – through exhibitions, performances, tours and concerts – just as ENSA, from its Drury Lane headquarters, was allocating 'shows of all types', as it called them, to troop units everywhere. Bell had spoken of 'spiritual values' (by which he meant something different from the Archbishop of York) and CEMA did its best (Bevin thought it 'too 'Ighbrow') not only to protect but to extend them. A propaganda film of 1942 introduced by R. A. Butler included, as part of the stilted dialogue: 'What's the point in all this here art? Pretty pictures don't win anything.' 'We all know what we're fighting against.' 'Don't you sometimes forget what we're fighting for?' 'Not pretty pictures.' 'Yes, but they're part of it.'

Fortunately not all the war pictures were pretty ones. The War Artists' Scheme established under Sir Kenneth Clark's chairmanship inspired some remarkable works of art – from Henry Moore's shelter drawings to Paul Nash's paintings of wrecked aircraft and John Piper's paintings of blitzed ruins. Nor was art an escape from danger or life. There is one unfinished painting in the War Artists' Collection in the Imperial War Museum damaged by shrapnel which actually killed the artist. And no one could say that an artist like Ardizzone forgot society.

At the same time, in painting as in music – and for that matter, in reading – people wanted to draw deeply not only on current inspiration but on the great works of all times, and the 'Picture of the Month' scheme, started in March 1942, was ushered in with Titian's *Noli me Tangere*, a not inappropriate title for those who did not wish everything to be touched by war. Likewise, the *Daily Telegraph Miscellany*, a highly successful anthology, showed in its introduction that 'the shocks of insolent challenges launched by Nazism and Fascism against not only Christianity but secular Morality' was fostering everywhere a demand for good literature.

Music too, while it was enlivened by new creative composers like Britten and Tippett, attracted the greatest audiences when it drew on past treasures. If Robert Donat turned as a listener to the unfailing solace of Bach, Myra Hess turned to it as a performer, and Kingsley Martin, for one, found what she played – mixing his musical media – 'the clear voice of reason in a crazy world!' *The Times* in its own way agreed. 'It's a good thing that someone is doing something about music. We need the rectifying influence which can stand for an immutable order of being unshaken by the shocks of politics.'

Before Russia came into the war, another *Times*, the *Croydon Times*, reminded its readers that in fairness to the memory of Tschaikovsky it should be explained that his music was the product of Tsarist and not Bolshevist Russia. But no-one bothered about such nice distinctions after Russia entered the war. There may have been doubts about the BBC playing the *Internationale* along with the national anthems of all the other allies, but Tschaikovsky and Shostakovitch were firmly placed in the same tradition which did *not* include Wagner. Julius Harrison, the Director of the Hastings Municipal Orchestra, had denied banning Wagner from his programmes in 1939 (although he omitted a few items 'because they might suggest the Siegfried Line'). Yet Wagner always had a raw deal, particularly with the BBC.

For most people during the war music meant not Bach and not even Tschaikovsky – but Vera Lynn and all the songs of the war (not usually about the war) which were sung by civilians at home and by the Forces overseas. *Calling the Forces Everywhere* broadcast from the Criterion (almost directly below Eros in Piccadilly Circus) was a basic part of the war effort and the 'Forces' Favourites' key people. It was *Melody Maker*, not Malcolm Sargent, which wrote in September 1939, 'Music comes right into its own in times of national menace. It is the main prop of the nation's morale.' (It went on to argue the case for 'reservation' of the country's best dance-band musicians on the grounds that their morale-boosting job should be considered as valuable war work.) 'South of the Border' was top of the hit parade with songs like 'They Can't Black-out the Moon' (not to speak of 'Sailor, Who are You Dreaming of Tonight?') still to come. Not surprisingly 'Long Ago and Far Away' belonged to 1944 which ended with Irving Berlin's 'White Christmas', the hit of all time. And we saw the war through in 1945 to 'We'll Gather Lilacs'.

There were to be no true successors during the Second World War, however, to the successful morale boosting songs of the First World War, 'gay and patriotic' (however strongly those who remembered that war – and some of those who managed the BBC – thought and argued that such songs were not only desirable but necessary for victory). 'Lili Marlene', taken over from the Germans, was rightly described by a radio commentator in 1943 as 'the one real song that the war has produced so far that can be compared with 'Tipperary' or 'Over There', and how different it was, whether sung by Lale Anderson, Anne Shelton or Vera Lynn.

The songs that were banned (like some of the comedian's gags) are just as interesting in retrospect as the songs that were plugged, even if few people at the time knew either of the bans or of the 'evils' of song plugging – a question was asked about the latter in the House of Commons in May 1940 with Reith, of all people, replying in his brief role as Minister of Information. Some of the oddest bans were imposed by the BBC after the Americans came into the war – 'Marching through Georgia' for example, because of Southern susceptibilities and 'Frankie and Johnnie'. Yet there were bans for domestic reasons too. Thus a song with the line 'Win-win-win-win with Churchill' was taboo because the lyric was considered unworthy of its subject. The American hit of 1944 'I Heard You Cried Last Night' was kept off the air because, as *Melody Maker* put it, 'a man crying was not a good thought at the present time'.

Dancing was always acceptable as wartime entertainment – though there were unsuccessful attempts to curb the new jitterbugging – in camps, cafes, town halls, dance halls, Sunday Schools, weekday schools, drawing rooms and kitchens. There were even tea dances with *Life* reporting in early 1941 that officers on leave in London could be seen 'taking their ladies' to the Piccadilly Hotel or to a Lyons Corner House, where eight-piece bands were playing 'The Rose of Tralee'. The BBC was broadcasting twenty dance band programmes a week in 1941, but Victor Silvester, whose *Dancing Club* was one of the most popular new radio programmes of the war, soon had an audience approximately twice that of any other band, presumably because people were actually dancing to him.

Outdoor life during the war was not taken over completely by allotment holders, pig clubs, and the Home Guard. Sport, amateur and professional, thrived though not without tribulations. After the first bans, soccer crowds were limited to fifteen thousand in 'safe' areas and eight thousand elsewhere, leagues were regionalized and the pools were 'pooled', but the game (and the pools) did not die. The Army and RAF elevens consisted almost entirely of internationals. The Board of Trade issued clothing coupons for football equipment, and Cardinal Hinsley, an improbable football fan, wrote in February 1940 that it would be 'an unspeakable [sic] blessing for mankind if national and international matters were organized on the plan of Association Football ... clean healthy sport.'

In November 1941, a correspondent to the *Sunday Times* – with racing more than football in mind – wrote that 'every effort should be made to keep sport going in this country on as big a scale as possible, for, if there is to be no sport, there will be no results to send out to our poor fellows (presumably prisoners of war) in Germany'. The Germans, of course, did not know about cricket, although Sir Pelham Warner (with strong Australian support) kept the Lords cricket ground inviolate during the war, arguing that if it were to be turned into something else Goebbels would be able to make 'valuable propaganda' out of it. Arsenal, by contrast, had turned their ground into a Civil Defence outpost, Twickenham and Hurlingham Polo Grounds were given over to allotments, and Home Guards drilled at Wimbledon. The Australian Prime Minister, John Curtin, who visited Lords twice in 1944, said happily that 'Australians will always fight for those twenty-two yards'.

Cricket, with its unofficial Test, stayed just as it was during the war. The golfers, however, were prepared to make wartime compromises. 'A ball removed by Enemy Action may be replaced as near as possible where it lay, or if lost or destroyed a ball may be dropped not nearer the hole without penalty.'

There were, of course, some non-believers in sport, just as there were in religion. Thus in May 1940 a group of people in Hythe (Kent), forgetting Sir Francis Drake, threatened to dig up the Borough Club's bowling green because they argued it was not right to play bowls in wartime. Yet the non-believers never won. The Penguin Special paperback by Archbishop Temple, *Christianity and Social Order*, sold 139,000 copies. (He had sent the proofs to J. M. Keynes for his comments.) In a survey made by Mass Observation at the end of the war, about two thirds of the people in a London suburb said that they believed in God although only four out of ten said that they ever went to Church. It was presumably, to quote an ITMA character, 'being so cheerful that kept them going', 'smiling through' while the war continued:

When you're up to your neck in hot water
Be like the kettle and sing.

The BBC, like the Windmill, never closed. Sandy Macpherson (*above*) played and played the BBC's theatre organ during the first weeks of the Phoney War, boring and inspiring many of his listeners. (He gave twenty-three broadcasts in the first week of war alone.) ITMA never ceased to entertain, with or without Mrs Mopp (*above right*). Arthur Askey and Richard Murdoch's famous flat at the top of Broadcasting House still attracted its official and unofficial visitors on Saturday 'Bandwaggon' nights (*right*). Singers, above all Vera Lynn (page 197), showed that they knew better than the BBC what people really wanted . . . although the idea behind the BBC's *Brains Trust* (*opposite below*) was copied in hundreds of towns where there was neither a Julian Huxley nor a Commander Campbell. Jack Warner (*opposite far right*) made his wartime way from the microphone to the advertisement.

the Grimness' ^(Title of the chapter on Variety in BBC Handbook, 1941)

"*Now, remember, nothing debilitated or anæmic.*"

JACK WARNER
THE NEW RADIO STAR

Did you MACLEAN your teeth to-day, Jack?

Yus, and my bruvver Syd.

BRAINS AT WORK

[The Brains Trust

COMMANDER CAMPBELL, MISS JENNIE LEE, DONALD McCULLOUGH, COLONEL WALTER ELLIOT,
DR. C. E. M. JOAD, DR. JULIAN HUXLEY

'The Greatest Show on Earth'

(Description of ENSA in official booklet, 1943)

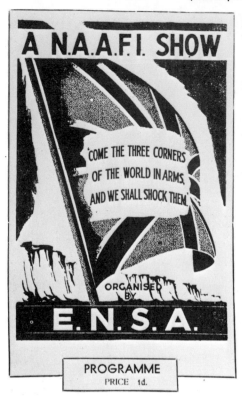

A N.A.A.F.I. SHOW

'COME THE THREE CORNERS OF THE WORLD IN ARMS, AND WE SHALL SHOCK THEM.'

ORGANISED BY

E.N.S.A.

PROGRAMME
PRICE 1d.

Every serviceman knew all about ENSA (and NAAFI). One in ten knew about CEMA. Yet the war promoted both entertainment (*above right* an ENSA concert) and the arts, even for people who did not understand what the initials stood for.

The Queen attended several of the National Gallery concerts organized by Myra Hess (*right*), although she was probably not among those who bought a sandwich for 3d. and sat on the floor. For Kingsley Martin, Dame Myra's first concert of Scarlatti sonatas 'seemed to reconstruct the exiled paintings'.

Programme of National Gallery concerts, week beginning October 16, 1939.
Monday at 1, Astra Desmond, May
   Harrison and Gerald Moore
Tuesday at 1 and 4.30, Moisevitsch
Wednesday at 1, Stratton String Quartet
Thursday at 1, Fleet Street Choir
Friday at 1 and 4.30, Antonio Brosa and
   William Murdoch
               Entrance 1s.

On the boards

(Above) *CEMA Canteen Concert, Isle of Dogs, London E14, 1941* by Kenneth Rowntree.
(Below) *An Afternoon Show by an ENSA Company in a NAAFI Canteen Hut, 1941*
by Frank Graves.

'Picture Parade'

Familiar features

'Everyone recognizes now,' wrote the film critic Roger Manvell at the end of the war, 'that there has been an extraordinary renaissance in British feature-film production since about 1940.' This page shows stills from three British wartime films: (*above*) Michael Balcon's *Let George Do It* (1940) with George Formby; (*below left*) *In Which We Serve* (1942) with Noel Coward; and (*above left*) *Millions Like Us* (1942) with (here) Patricia Roc.

Cinema forms varied, with 'shorts' and a regular flow of full-length feature war films beginning with *The Lion has Wings* (which opened with the commentator proudly announcing, 'This is England where we believe in freedom.'). By 1941 *Life* reported the British preferred 'service heroes' to Clark Gable, but this, like many other such statements, was not entirely true, as the continuing success of *Gone with the Wind* showed. There was always a market for escape, *The Man in Grey* rather than the man in khaki, and Churchill's favourite film, *Lady Hamilton*.

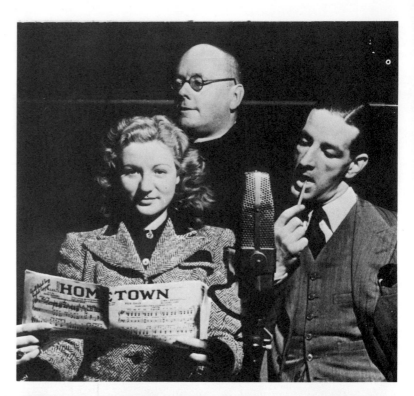

Theatres and cinemas (closed when war broke out) soon re-opened. George Bernard Shaw described their early closure as 'a master-stroke of unimaginative stupidity', conveniently forgetting that the Home Office did not know if and when the great air attack would come.

The BBC strengthened its links with stage and cinema as transatlantic show-biz brought 'Nice People', as *Melody Maker* described Ben Lyon and Bebe Daniels, to Britain. Their show *Hi Gang!* (which also starred Vic Oliver, Churchill's son-in-law) (*above*) and singers like Anne Shelton (*above right*) were broadcast not only to Britain but to thousands of listeners overseas. Tommy Trinder, backed by chorus girls, was appearing in a film with the least glamorous of all wartime titles, *Communal Kitchen* (*right*). Other titles also had their incongruities. Thus, *Sandbag Follies* at the Unity Theatre (members only) was described as 'a tonic for democrats'.

and games

The theatre could be a place of danger as well as of entertainment (*above left* a shattered safety curtain at the Holborn Empire). When war broke out, *Band Waggon* was being filmed at Gainsborough Studios. It was immediately halted on the grounds that the huge power chimney might collapse during an air raid and crush everybody. (It was later completed at pre-BBC Lime Grove.) It drew huge audiences to the theatre, too, Jack Hylton presenting (*below left*).

Theatre audiences had been warned personally at first by anxious managers that they ought to leave when air raids started. Later they became blasé (even in the age of V1s and V2s) and barely read the notices printed in their programmes (*above*) before deciding *not* to leave, whether they were watching light entertainment or Shakespeare (complete with Olivier and Gielgud).

Sport could be dangerous too. One of the few photographs of a wartime cricket match shows players at Lords lying on the ground as a doodlebug passed overhead. Pictures of wartime football matches look deceptively like any others – apart from a sprinkling of tin hats and gas masks among players and spectators.

Diversions

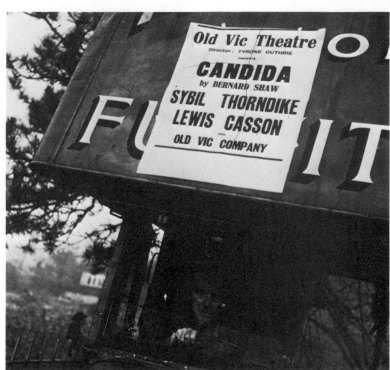

The name of Gracie Fields, according to a BBC report 'Listening in France' in early 1940, 'was on many occasions bracketed with that of Mr Winston Churchill as a popular turn'. (*Right*) 'Our Gracie' appeared with Maurice Chevalier (later to be condemned as a semi-collaborator) at a Gala Performance in Drury Lane just before France fell. Edith Evans's famous monologue, *The Hop-Picker* (*above*), originally featured in a Farjeon review, *Diversions* (the title a pun on police notices diverting traffic around unexploded bombs), which played to full houses in Charing Cross Road every afternoon in the spring of the Blitz, 1941. Backed by CEMA funds, the Old Vic made triumphant tours of South Wales mining towns and northern industrial cities. (*Above right*) Lewis Casson at the wheel of the company van.

But the arts had enemies too: the *Daily Express* declared 'The Government gives £50,000 to help wartime culture. What sort of madness is this? There is no such thing as culture in wartime.'

'We never closed'

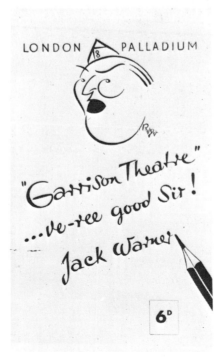

The Windmill was (briefly) at the height of the Blitz the only theatre open in London and its showgirls (*above*) became symbols of courage as well as of sex. *Garrison Theatre* (*left*), described by the BBC in 1939 (in its radio version) as 'a music hall programme with trimmings,' was based on the producer, Harry S. Pepper's memories of a real First World War garrison theatre. Its star, Jack Warner, summed up the early days of the war with his traditional blue pencil jokes, and catch phrases, 'Mind My Bike', 'a rill mill' and 'di-da-di-da'. The BBC's *Happidrome* also depended on catch phrases ('Let me tell you', 'Take 'im away Ramsbottom') and everyone knew its theme song, 'We Three'. Like all successful radio shows, *Happidrome* transferred to the stage. (*Far left*) 1942 theatre programme.

'It's Foolish But It's Fun'

(1943 musical)

Two great partnerships: Jack Hulbert and Cecily Courtneidge (*above*) with Ronald Shiner in *Something in the Air*, a popular musical of 1943 and Nervo and Knox of the Crazy Gang (who were said to run the Ministry of Information during daylight hours).

'Workers' Playtime'

'Rest from work has become a precious thing – and, because the quality of work depends so largely upon it, one of great value to the nation,' ponderously (but sensibly) asserted the BBC Handbook in 1942. Minister of Labour Ernest Bevin agreed, giving his blessing in 1941 to holiday camps for war-workers (*left*) and to shows like *Workers' Playtime*: 'I have to do so much directing, constructing and exhorting that it's a pleasure to spend a few moments introducing you to something on the lighter side.' (*Above*) 'Wartime Blackpool 1942. The dancers who reached the end of the pier. They paid to get in. They struggled to get along. Now they've managed to elbow a way onto the floor. They can carry on from dawn till dusk, once they've got there.' (Contemporary caption to photograph)

'Saturday night at the Palais'

The artistic 'virility' of the popular crooner 'Hutch' was questioned by BBC officials during the anti-slush campaign of 1942. (*Right*) Lou Preager, famous dance band leader, at the Hammersmith Palais. (*Below*) Covent Garden Mecca.

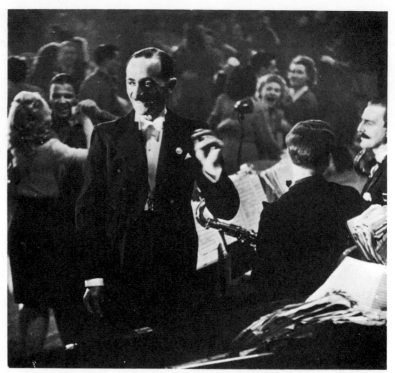

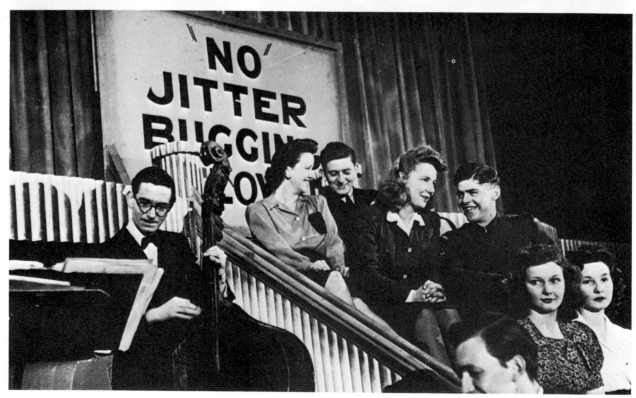

'Happy and Glorious'

(Title of London Palladium show, *below*)

Whilst Hitler was describing jazz as 'a barbaric and bestial music of the sub-human Negro exploited by Jewish Capitalists', British dancers enjoyed the new jitterbugging – in camps, cafés, town halls, dance halls, Sunday Schools, week-day schools, drawing rooms and kitchens. There were even tea dances with *Life* reporting in early 1941 that officers on leave in London could be seen 'taking their ladies' to the Piccadilly Hotel or to a Lyons Corner House, where eight piece bands were playing 'The Rose of Tralee'. The BBC was broadcasting twenty dance band programmes a week in 1941, but Victor Silvester, whose Dancing Club was one of the most popular new radio programmes of the war, soon had an audience approximately twice as that for another band, presumably because people were actually dancing to him. For those who did not dance there were always showgirls to watch at the Palladium (*above*) and at the cabaret (*left*).

'She's a woman, that's what she is!

(Mrs Mopp)

THE SAME FROCK

1939 **1940**

NOTE !

Many think that a Garment can only be Dyed to a darker shade.

Clark's can Dye any Garment to practically *any* shade.

AUTUMN FROCKS PLUS-DYED A *LIGHTER* SHADE FOR SPRING

Here's a typical Spring budget—see what you save !

Town Coat	16/3	2 Day Frocks	13/6
Swagger Coat	9/-	3 Jumpers	18/-
Evening Gown	12/-	Total	£3/3/0

(including Speciality Fashion Colours)

Formal fashion came to a virtual standstill during the war. In 1944 Anne Scott James wrote in *Picture Post*, 'Buying clothes is a responsible business when every coupon counts . . . in these days of shortage choose classics every time.' *Vogue* applauded 'the Queen who in spite of the pressure of uniformity, never herself appears in uniform, but continues to charm us with highly personal, exquisite clothes'. By *not* following fashion the Queen was said patriotically to have made do throughout the war with the wardrobe she took on a foreign tour in early 1939. Her subjects had to mend as well as make-do ('a stitch in time saves – coupons'; 'plus-fours would make two pairs of shorts for a schoolboy').
(*Right*) Black market cosmetics maker.

216

'You confirm my worst suspicions'

(Tommy Handley, ITMA, 1942)

1942-43 CLOTHING BOOK

This book may not be used until the holder's name, full postal address and National Registration (Identity Card) Number have been plainly written below IN INK.

NAME_____
(BLOCK LETTERS)

ADDRESS_____
(BLOCK LETTERS)

(TOWN)_____ (COUNTY)_____

NATIONAL REGISTRATION (IDENTITY CARD) NUMBER

Read the instructions within carefully, and take great care not to lose this book
Page 1

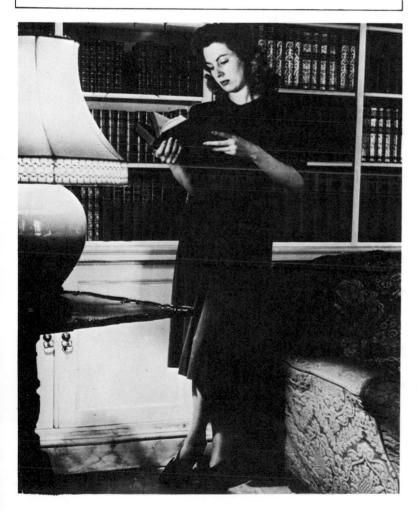

Churchill disliked the idea of clothes rationing, introduced in June 1941, but Mass Observation found that the British people were seven to one in its favour. The basic rate of 66 coupons was intended to cover one complete outfit a year and in 1942 *Housewife* commented, 'Slowly the essence of our attitude towards clothes has changed. Now at the end of our third year of war a bandbox reputation is not only unimportant but undesirable.' But fashionable instincts – if not their practice – survived austerity, with reports from the *Manchester Guardian* that 'a waist in wartime seems an anomaly, but less so than when accompanied by hips and busts', and the encouraging news from *Woman's Fair* that 'the perfect bust points slightly upwards, but even slightly weary busts can now cry Excelsior and there are just seven things you can do about it.'

Despite the women's new wartime jobs and responsibilities, old attitudes died hard. This 1943 song lyric sums up the ideal (unliberated) middle-class wife, home-maker and morale-booster par excellence:

'Good Morning, my sweet',
I say to my Brenda,
She cares for my home
And I'd die to defend her.
She mends my old vests
And she takes out the pup
And she sees to the kids
Now that Nanny's called up
She checks up the laundry
And flatters the cook
Then she goes to the library
And gets me a book
Her housekeeping money
Is twelve bob in credit
That ration book form is OK
For she's read it
She's vamped our old grocer
And brought back a tin
Of sardines and some cheese
And a bottle of gin
She's a pearl of a wife
No man could have better
So I kiss her good morning
And then I forget her.

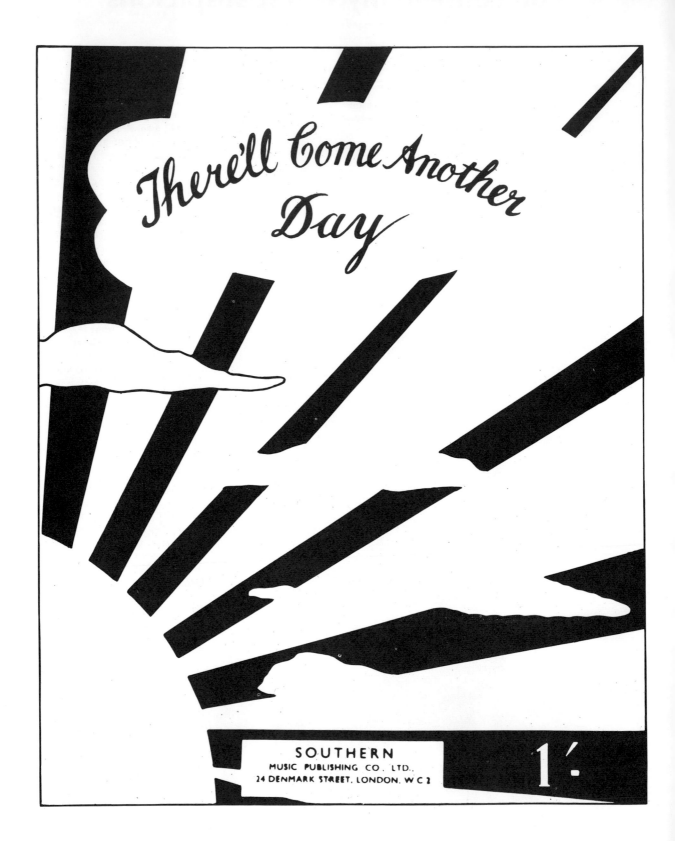

IT'S A LOVELY DAY TOMORROW

"MY GOODNESS, MY HAPPINESS!"

With apologies to Guinness & Co.

It's a lovely day tomorrow
Tomorrow is a lovely day
Come and feast your tear-dimmed eyes
On tomorrow's clear blue skies . . .
Tomorrow is a lovely day.

Whatever the BBC might do to ban 'crying through', even some of the songs of hope could not avoid phrases like 'tear-dimmed eyes'. You could not be cheerful all the time during a war, even with Mrs Mopp's example, and if nothing else could or would rally you, visions of the bright future after the war might. It was not the Trades Unions Congress but the Federation of British Industries which predicted in May 1942 that 'we are on the threshold of a new world, and the theories and practices of the past cannot be taken for granted in the future'. It was *The Times* not the *Daily Mirror* which wrote later in the same year, after the publication of the Beveridge Report on Social Security, that 'this decisive epoch' needed 'a great social measure which will go far towards restoring the faith of ordinary men and women throughout the world in the power of democracy'.

Churchill believed that the 'power of democracy' should be used to crush Hitler and that until Hitler had been crushed all dreaming was daydreaming. And he had his supporters. 'With respect to war aims', *Everybody's Weekly* remarked in the year when the Federation of British Industries and *The Times* were both looking ahead to the world *after* the war, 'it is useless to talk vaguely of new orders or of making the World safe for democracy. The job our statesmen are paid to do is to see that the World, as God made it, is safe for Great Britain.'

The difficulty about such statements – even before the tides of war turned – was that the world was not just as God made it, particularly the world of the 1930s. The experience of the 'bitter society', as Professor Marwick has called it, turned people towards the vision of the better society. Indeed, Churchill himself had been as eloquent as anyone else – in the Atlantic Charter of 1941 – about the necessity to make 'the world safe for democracy',

and the Labour members of his Cabinet (an important presence in this context) had insisted that a reference to social welfare should be incorporated in it. In an exchange of royal letters – from Queen Elizabeth to Queen Mary in 1940 – the young Queen wrote to the old, 'I feel quite exhausted after seeing and hearing so much sadness, sorrow, heroism and magnificent spirit. The destruction is so awful, and the people so *wonderful* – they deserve a better world.'

For a whole number of reasons which some of the leader writers on *The Times* (particularly E. H. Carr) well knew, 'democracy' during the war was coming to mean 'social democracy'. The very conception of wartime 'solidarity' – related to the war effort and to the common struggle against physical insecurity – could easily be transferred to the peace effort and to future common struggles against social insecurity. Even 'utility' styles – and still more the sales talk to popularize them – suggested a kind of 'war socialism' and the end of luxury (although perhaps the beginning of good 'pure' design for all). Finally the appeal to the younger generation, on whom the actual fighting depended, had to be couched in the language of the future. 'In the youth of the nation we have our greatest asset,' said the Board of Education platitudinously (it might have added the babies), and it was as much out of platitudes (if in bleak peacetime they had not always been recognized as such), as out of principles that new welfare policies were being forged. These policies, which covered health as well as education, were to be fully implemented and systematized after 1945.

'They don't expect the millennium,' Howard Marshall, skilled pre-war broadcaster, said of troops in wartime. 'They do expect a fair deal.' And he said it to the man for whom he had been working in wartime, Lord Woolton, who ceased to be Minister of Food in November 1943 and became Minister of Reconstruction. 'Reconstruction' had been the in-word in 1917, and Woolton had developed the 'fair shares for all' food policy.

Lord Woolton, a future Chairman of the Conservative Party, took it for granted from the start that there would have to be full employment, building controls to produce more houses, and a new educational system (though he thought of 'ladders' as well as common 'respect for work'). Yet he believed – and this set him apart from idealists – that 'thinking is a more laborious exercise than hoping'. The British were to lack food in the years of continuing austerity after 1945, but Lord Woolton was willing to offer them every other kind of consolation at his disposal.

It was not only politicians, however, who could think. A Somerset housewife describing the VJ celebrations in August 1945 reflected that 'in spite of the joy one can't help reflecting that our larders are bare, there are no houses for our returning soldiers . . . Everyone's house needs painting and replastering, our clothes are shabby, and one can't buy a sheet or a blanket unless one is bombed-out or newly-wed . . . Life is going to be every bit as strenuous; we are all exhausted . . . The best minute of the day has been just to sit down and realize that the war is over.'

In that very distant future – for so it seemed in 1942 – Churchill was not to be Prime Minister. He had not found the right political language for 1945. In 1942 and 1943, however, he was prepared to try. He reverted naturally – as might have been expected – to some of his 'hoping' of the Edwardian period in the 'dear dead days beyond recall', talking, for example, as he might have done in 1908 of the Beveridge Report 'bringing the magic of averages to the rescue of the millions'. In a 'Four Year Plan' broadcast of 21 March 1942, in which he said that he approved of 'putting milk into babies' (one of the great social achievements of the year of Dunkirk), he deliberately referred to his past in the struggle for the national insurance scheme of 1911.

The 'millions' had ideas of their own, and few of them looked back as far as 1908 or 1911. They were encouraged to think as well as to hope not only by many of the newspapers and the BBC but by unofficial bodies like the Workers' Educational Association and by the official Army Bureau of Current Affairs. The cinema, too, played its part in diffusing the hopes. Thus, in *Dawn Guard* (script

by Roy Boulting, 1941) one Home Guard (Bernard Miles) tells another (Percy Walsh) that it wasn't enough just 'to stop Hitler'. 'We've made a fine big war effort and after it's all over, we've got to make a fine big peace effort . . . There must be no more chaps hanging around for work that doesn't come – no more slums neither – no more filthy dirty back streets – no more half-starved kids with no room to play in – we got to pack all of that up and get moving into the brightness of the sun.' It had to be a Lovely Day Tomorrow, 'We found out in this war as how we were all neighbours, and we aren't going to forget it when it's all over. That's how you say it – "The old men shall see visions, and the young men shall dream dreams."'

The dreams and the visions were not always remote and Utopian: sometimes they were directly inspired by the exigencies of war. Thus when the poet Louis MacNeice (also a distinguished writer of radio scripts) reported for *Picture Post* on the London Blitz in May 1941, he commented that as he saw the buildings still burning or being demolished the morning after a bad raid 'there was a voice inside me which (ignoring all the suffering and wastage involved) kept saying: "Let her go up!" or "Let her come down. Let them all go. Write them all off. Stone walls do not a city make. Tear all the blotted pages out of the book . . ."' Jerome Willis, the *Evening Standard* reporter, drew social as well as architectural morals from London's bomb damage, reflecting that 'bombs had brought out sharply the difference in the way the classes lived . . . I wondered then if those citizens who stayed to work in the stricken capital would have much of a voice in the promised post-war economic changes, or would those who owned most of it, but had stayed very far away from it when the bombs were falling, come back again to reign?'

Bombs were levellers – as the King and Queen had found when Buckingham Palace was bombed. Churchill himself had written to the King: 'The war has drawn the Throne and the people more closely together than was ever before recorded, and Your Majesties are more beloved by all classes and conditions than any princes of the past'. A more humble – although equally articulate – Blitz victim said in a broadcast now in the BBC Archives:

'When I arrived out of that shelter on the Saturday morning, the doors of which happened to be red hot, by the way, and twenty-one of us in that shelter – I found that station, name and everything had vanished along with the smoke of the bomb, and we had arrived at a stage that I as one person had always looked for – a stage of equality, a stage of no snobbery, a stage whereby here we met as human beings, sympathetic . . . when we never were sympathetic before . . .'

The experience of evacuation had the same effect on thoughtful people, like an idealistic Southampton schoolmaster, evacuated with his school to a Somerset village, who wrote: 'all of them (the evacuees) will have gained an experience and a broadened outlook which will inevitably modify their future lives . . . A deeper understanding will, I hope, arise between the peoples of our own land and perhaps this evacuation may go on for this purpose even when war no longer demands it.' At a more practical level, evacuation, by revealing town to country, poor to rich, rowdy to respectable, gave Britain a new dimension of self-knowledge, and aroused a new sense of social concern.

"What was the post-war world like after the last war?"

'Our dreams were getting better all the time.' For some intellectuals – from the very beginning – they had been dreams of Europe. For most people, however, they were dreams not even of Britain, but of Exeter or Leeds or Selkirk . . . and particular streets and particular people in them . . . localized dreams centring on particular jobs, homes, towns, villages. There were, of course, a few like Harold Nicolson – he was even to stand unsuccessfully as a Labour candidate after the war – who regretted the end of 'les douceurs de la vie'. 'We shall have to walk and live a Woolworth life hereafter,' he wrote in his diary in June 1941. 'I hate the destruction of elegance.' Charles Ritchie, with his Canadian background, also reacted privately against the meanness and austerity of wartime. In December 1941 he wrote in his diary:

'Oh God, leave us our luxuries even if we must do without our necessities. Let Cartier's and the Ritz be restored to their former glories. Let house-parties burgeon once more in the stately homes of England. Restore the vintage port to the clubs and the old brown sherry to the colleges. Let us have pomp and luxury, painted jezebels and scarlet guardsmen, – rags and riches rubbing shoulders. Give us back our bad, old world.'

Ritchie hoped himself that 'the sober reasonable socialism of the future' would not imply 'the disappearance of distinction' or of 'pleasant ornamental amusing people and things'. He was wrong, however, when he referred to 'the austere prospect of cotton stockings'. Nylon was to see to that.

The war gave a great stimulus to science and technology – and to medicine. And here, there seemed to be hope based on thought and reason . . . facts not fancy. Government expenditures on the Department of Scientific and Industrial Research and the Medical Research Council had as their main object 'supplying quick answers to practical questions as they arose', but it was known that scientists were interested in other questions too, and that some of them, at least, had long-term views. The Medical Research Council itself in an official report spoke of bringing future 'benefit to mankind under conditions of peace'. In a *Picture*

Post article in January 1944, Walter Elliott, Minister of Health, picked as the best news of 1943 not Stalingrad but the discovery of penicillin. What was not known – even to Attlee – was that a large part of the scientific effort was being directed to the atomic bomb – and that some of the hopes of the future, therefore, were to be chilled with Hiroshima and Nagasaki after VE-Day.

The British themselves had been reminded during the last stages of the war – with the VI and V2 attacks – not only that 'secret weapons' existed but that science and technology had two faces. Rocketry (though it was not to be identified so clearly as such) was as much a by-product of war as computers (also not so identified) or radar, and it was to make thoughts of how to wage global war in the future so sophisticated that only scientists could understand them. In 1939 people still looked back to 1914–18, although they had feared the new image of war. After 1945 the images were new ones and there were to be no acknowledged precedents. Out of 'clear blue skies' who knew what would come?

We've great things to do

The Atlantic Charter

1. Britain and the United States seek no territorial or other aggrandizement.

2. No territorial changes that do not accord with the freely expressed wishes of the peoples concerned.

3. Respect for the right of all peoples to choose their own form of Government and restoration of sovereign rights and self-government to those forcibly deprived of them.

4. They will endeavour, with due respect for their existing obligations, to further the enjoyment by all States, great or small, victor or vanquished, of access, on equal terms, to the trade and to the raw materials of the world which are needed for their prosperity.

5. Full collaboration among nations in the economic field aimed at improved labour standards, economic advancement and social security.

6. After the final destruction of the Nazi tyranny, they hope to see established a peace which will afford to all nations the means of dwelling in safety within their own boundaries and which will afford assurance that all the men in all the lands may live out their lives in freedom from fear and want.

7. Freedom of the seas for all nations.

8. Abandonment of the use of force, and disarmament of nations which threaten, or may threaten aggression outside of their frontiers pending establishment of a wider and permanent system of general security.

. and Comrades

CAIRO REUNION 1955

"REMEMBER THAT MAN—HITLER ?"

In August 1941 Churchill met Roosevelt at Placentia Bay, Newfoundland, where they drew up the Joint Declaration on War Aims whose eight points were known as the Atlantic Charter (*opposite*). The reference to social security was said to have been included only after pressure from Ernest Bevin.

A dream that did not come true (*left*). By 1955 Roosevelt and Stalin were both dead.

The entrance of Russia into the war on the Allied side sparked off enthusiasm for Russia. The Russian Ambassador, Mr Maisky, recorded 'infinite and unquestionable' admiration for Russia among 'the masses' (an attitude expressed by this 1942 Communist Party poster (*above*): the ban on the *Daily Worker* was lifted in September 1942). Maisky's 'ruling classes' were equally pro-Russian for a time. Mrs Churchill herself sponsored the Aid to Russia Fund.

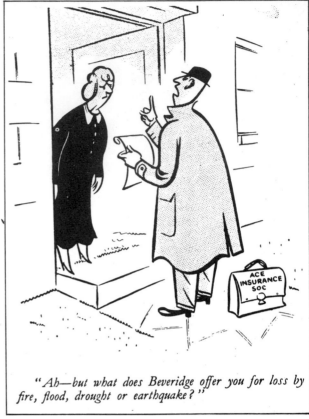

"*Ah—but what does Beveridge offer you for loss by fire, flood, drought or earthquake?*"

Those who prate about a better social order after the war are talking mischievous nonsense,' wrote Dean Inge in the *Evening Standard* in November 1940 – *after* Dunkirk. 'However the war ends, we shall be an impoverished nation. We shall all have to work harder and spend less.' Dean Inge might have been happy with the victory of the Cross over the swastika, but Beveridge offered full employment and social security for all. 'Freedom from want cannot be forced on a democracy. It must be won by them . . . in this supreme crisis the British people will not be found wanting of courage and faith and national unity, of material and spiritual power . . .'

A soldier embarking for D-Day put it more simply. 'Ernie, when we have done this job for you, are we going back on the dole?'

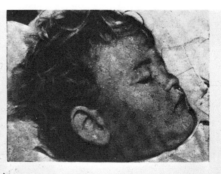

Do you want him taught to hate you?

He could be—if the Nazis caught him young enough. He might be — if you gave them the chance.

Impossible? But it's happening now, the other side of the Channel. Little children are taught to despise the "softness" of home life, to worship the "Party" alone. That is why you read of parents betrayed to the Gestapo by their darlings — and children made proud of such "service to the State."

Cruel? But so is the Nazi creed; the creed they would hasten to force upon us whom they hate most of all.

We must not allow them to steal our children's souls.

Save more — lend more, and do it quickly. Have you anything one half so precious as that tranquil look in mother's eye, the happy trustful talk and laughter that make what we call "home"?

★   ★   ★
Put every penny you can scrape together into — War Savings!

. but Victory first

LOVE ME, LOVE MY DOG

The first real effort to organize moral resistance on a European front was made in the V for Victory campaign, launched in January, 1941: 'You in Europe who listen to me now, you are the unknown soldiers. The Nazi official and the German soldier don't know you, but they fear you. The night is your friend, the 'V' is your sign, and it's beginning to play on their nerves. There's a "V" sound – here's the letter V in morse.' ('Colonel Britton' broadcast, BBC Archive Disc)

The campaign was rapidly absorbed into British folk lore (*below left* patriotic London flower seller). 'V for Victory' was chalked up on walls everywhere and one Welsh Bethel Temple even displayed a sign saying 'CalVary'. The *Liverpool Echo* reported in November 1941 that a baby girl had been born in New South Wales with a 'V' in the centre of her forehead and a record review in the *Airscrew* recommended: 'Debroy Somers and his Band, V (. . . ▁) Symphony (Abridged Version), Columbia DX1028. One of Beethoven's liveliest works. A grand piece, with victory emphasised throughout.'

For many good democrats victory alone was not enough. In July 1940 Harold Nicolson wrote warningly: 'The Germans are fighting a revolutionary war for very definite objectives. We are fighting a conservative war and our objectives are purely negative. We must put forward a positive and revolutionary aim admitting that the old order has collapsed and asking people to fight for the new order.'

'I am worried about this damned election. I have no message for them now.' (Churchill to his doctor, June 1945) Many people felt that Churchill as the 'National Leader' was overshadowed by the interests of the Conservative Party, and this issue led to the Conservative defeat in 1945. (*Above left* Vicky's cartoon in *News Chronicle*, 23 May 1945)

'Bombs have made builders of us all'

(*Journal of Federation of British Industries*, October 1940)

'Prefabrication', the government's sensible answer to the housing problem, soon acquired a sinister new meaning. 'People have got the idea it means jerry-building, tumble-down shacks, caravans, shoddy work, ribbon development, draughts, leaks and everything that's bad in buildings,' wrote *Picture Post* in 1944. It need not have meant any of these things: only the execution, not the idea, was at fault.

Prefabrication was the only way Britain might have provided the four million houses needed after the war. When even the Government seemed to think that prefabrication meant something temporary it was not surprising that newspapers carried reports like this: 'Four-room bungalows costing about £130 each, are to be proposed as temporary homes for bombed out people. As these bungalows would not be a satisfactory form of housing in a post-war era, it will be suggested that they be utilised for old age pensioners after the war.' (*Daily Mirror*, 1941)

" *Progress or no, somebody'll* ALWAYS *crop up with roots in the past . . .*"

'All that you see . . . is pure, it's good'

(Edwin Clinch, one of the designers of Utility Furniture)

" You'll have to do something to this room to match your Utility furniture."

For five years I've dreamed about my new home—

And as every woman will understand, most of my dreams have been about the kitchen I'd have. How I'm looking forward to my Acme! No wash-day terrors for me, with a wringer that's so easy to use and so easy on the clothes, too. I've seen blankets put through an Acme, and frail little baby clothes, too — and both come out just perfect.

Great news! The day when your dream will come true is drawing near. Soon now new, better-than-ever Acmes will be at your dealers. Lose no time! Be sure that you are among the first to get one of the new Acmes, for the whitest washes and the easiest wash-days you have ever known

In 1945 the *Architectural Review* commented on the good effects of the war on design . . . 'It was pushed back to essentials because there was no room for waste of materials and manpower in production.' Scientists, designers and production experts co-operated to fulfil the brief of Hugh Dalton, President of the Board of Trade, 'to produce specifications for furniture of good, sound construction in simple but agreeable designs for reasonable prices, and ensuring the maximum economy of raw materials and labour'.

Gordon Russell, the furniture designer, wrote in 1946, 'I felt that to raise the whole standard of furniture for the mass of the people was not a bad war job.'

'The Apotheosis of Austerity'

(Title of *Vogue* feature on the first Utility Fashions, October 1942)

In 1942 the Civilian Clothing Order (Utility motif *above*) introduced Utility clothes. Top London couturiers like Hardy Amies, Norman Hartnell (whose 1943 designs for Berkertex are shown on this page) and Digby Morton co-operated with the Board of Trade's request to provide designs for four specified basic outfits. *Vogue* welcomed the new 'Couture Utility Designs' (October 1942): 'Now, the woman in the street, the next strap-hanger in the 'bus, the parcel-carrier and the pram-pusher, the government clerk and the busy housewife will all have an equal chance to buy beautifully designed clothes, suitable to their lives and incomes. It is a revolutionary scheme and a heartening thought. It is in fact, an outstanding example of applied democracy.'

'Heard about the Utility woman? She's single-breasted.' (Wartime joke)

Variations on a theme

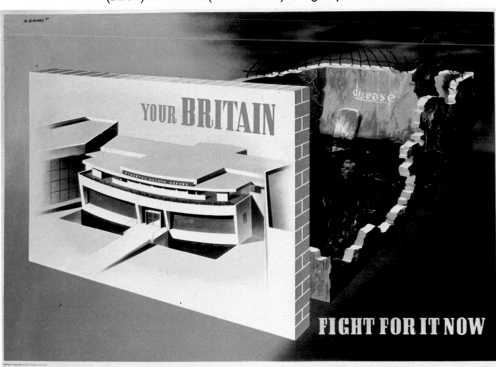

Two 1942 ABCA posters. (*Above*) Traditional poster by Frank Newbould.
(*Below*) Surrealist (and socialist) design by Abram Games.

Sweet dreams

"That's Gilchrist—in charge of post-war planning."

WHEN THE LIGHTS GO ON AGAIN

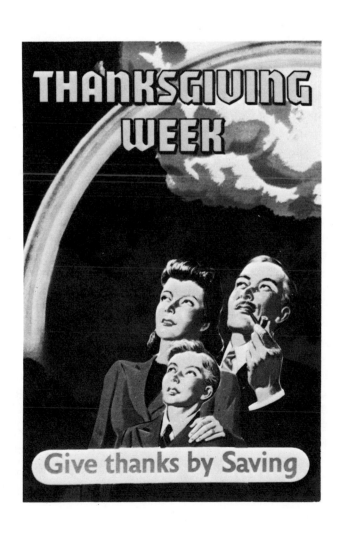

*When the lights go on again all over the world
And the boys are home again all over the world
And rain or snow is all that may fall from skies
    above
A kiss won't mean 'Goodbye' but 'Hello' to love.*

The end of a six-year war is bound to be dramatic –
a great event in itself, public and private. 'Hurry
up please it's time', T. S. Eliot had written in
The Waste Land (1922) after a shorter war. During
the Second World War, however, there was some
light in the tunnel for many months before the
lights went on again . . . first in Britain and Europe,
and then, far more quickly than had been anticipated, all over the world.

D-Day was the necessary preliminary to V-Day,
and D-Day itself was preceded by elaborate preparations, kept well secret. It was followed, too,
by what Churchill called 'the hour of our greatest
effort'. 'The only homeward road for all of us,' he
went on, 'lies through the arch of victory.' One of
the signs that the effort was now converging at
last on Hitler's Germany was the 'half regretful' dis-
banding of the Home Guard in September 1944 . . .
the army which, in the proud words of *Picture
Post*, 'knew what democracy meant'. It was the
army, also, of course, 'that never had to fight'.

There were setbacks as well as victories in store
in 1944 and 1945 for the armies that were fighting
their way towards Germany (the final 'encircle-
ment' that had so long figured in Nazi mythology
and propaganda), and between D-Day and VE-Day
there was to be one last unexpected German
assault on war-weary England itself. A week after
D-Day on 12 June the first VI pilotless plane
crossed the English coast, and during the following
months about eight thousand were launched
against London and 2,400 fell in Kent. For a time
the letter V stood not for Victory but for Ven-
geance (*Vergeltung*). On 8 September, four years
after the great Battle of Britain, the longer-range
V2s began to fall out of the autumn sky. They fell
too late to win the war, but civilians once again
found themselves in the main line of attack. There
is a London story, one of hundreds from the period,
about Mrs Smith being bombed out of the ruins of
a London street struck by a V2. Fortunately she
was found conscious and not seriously injured, and
a member of the WVS began to take down her
record. Had she a husband? Yes, she had a husband.
Where was her husband? 'He's at the front, the
dirty coward,' Mrs Smith replied.

There were ten thousand casualties in the first
week of the VIs, and though the VIs soon began to
be passed off lightly as 'doodlebugs', which Harold
Nicolson, for one, called 'a perfectly secondary
and useless form of attack', the V2s, which gave no
warning, were more sinister. (At first the Government pretended they were exploding gas-mains, a
story which convinced no-one.) 'If I'm going to be
killed', one lady (quoted by Mollie Panter-Downes)
remarked, 'I would like to have the excitement of
knowing it's going to happen.'

After D-Day everyone knew, of course, despite
VIs, V2s and the Ardennes offensive, what was
going to happen on the 'homeward road', though
no one knew when . . . and it was not until 26
March 1945 that the last V2 fell (as apocalyptically
as any) on the Whitfield Tabernacle in Tottenham
Court Road. 'No bombs, ain't it lovely?' Vere
Hodgson wrote in her diary a few days later.

At least you did not need to tighten the blackout to deal with those new unmanned invaders from the skies, although there was a new evacuation, some theatres closed and the Headmasters of Eton and Harrow cancelled the Eton and Harrow match. Prophets noted that Dr Samuel Johnson, whose London house was destroyed by a VI, had asked in *Rasselas* 'What would be the security of the good if the bad could at pleasure invade them from the skies? . . . Neither walls, nor mountains, nor seas could afford any security.'

". . . and what is a doodle-bug?"

The first V2s had not been identified for the general public, when on 17 September 1944 the blackout gave way to the dim-out. Some people called it the wash-out, and even *The Times* said it made little difference to the West End. Yet although a full blackout was re-imposed for a time later, the dim-out meant that it was now possible to use 'curtains and blinds of the kind . . . normally fitted before the War' if you still had any. Sticky tape on windows went out before red tape as lighting on buses and trains was restored to 'normal'. On Christmas Day 1944 churches could light their stained glass windows, and two days after Christmas (as the news came in on the radio of the surprising German Ardennes offensive) car headlight masks were abolished. It was not until 20 April 1945, however, that Herbert Morrison finally announced the end of the blackout to the cheers of MPs and to the alarm of some young children, who, it was claimed, were terrified of the unfamiliar bright lights.

The brightest lights were still banned not to save lives but to save fuel. You could not, for example, floodlight piers or bandstands. Many freedoms were revived, however, between D-Day and VE-Day. You could now buy a large-scale map, use a car radio, sleep in an uncamouflaged tent, sound a factory hooter, even release a racing pigeon without police permission. It was not until after the war had ended however, that Parliament repealed (without any delay) the Act making the spreading of alarm and despondency a punishable offence. 'Now,' wrote Vere Hodgson, 'we can be as unhappy as we please. Freedom is returning.' The 'free hearts' could worry about new things as well as sing about the old and the new.

The film *Diary for Timothy* (1945) put this theme somewhat differently. The baby Timothy of the title was born on 3 September 1944. 'Life will become more dangerous than before, oddly enough', was the message for him as prepared by the scriptwriter, 'more dangerous because we have now the power to choose, the right to criticize and even to grumble. We're free men, we have to decide for ourselves.'

Memories of 'the worst war ever known' intermingled in 1944 and 1945 – death could still arrive by telegram – with hopes for the future. Yet VE-Day itself was a day neither for the Past nor for the Future but for the Present. 'The whole of Trafalgar Square,' wrote Harold Nicolson, 'was packed with people. Somebody had made a corner in rosettes, flags, streamers, paper whisks and above all, paper caps. The latter were horrible, being of the comic variety. I also regret to say that I observed three Guardsmen in full uniform wearing such hats.'

They were not the only people to cast care aside on a day when there was both 'comic variety' and unqualified delight that the long European war had ended in what the King called 'a great deliverance'. The Board of Trade had announced solemnly just before that until the end of May you could buy cotton bunting without coupons, 'as long as it is red, white or blue and does not cost more than one and three a square yard'. To the horror of Nat Gubbins, some people seemed to have been better prepared for V-Day in 1945 than the country had been for war in 1939. In *Dialling TUM* he wrote, 'You could hardly expect an event like that to pass without celebrations.'

'No, I suppose not.'

'In fact the celebrations might go on for a week. Or even a fortnight.'

'Oh Lord.'

'Don't be defeatist. To be forewarned is to be forearmed.'

'I seem to have heard that before.'

Light was as much a feature of the celebrations as fire had been of the Blitz. People talked of the 'Torch of Victory', and as 'The lights were going on again everywhere' it was hoped that they would remain bright for many a generation. One of the floodlit buildings was Buckingham Palace, where the Royal Family appeared with Churchill on the balcony. Another was Broadcasting House, floodlit for the first time since Coronation Day, 1937. It was the back streets, however, which waved the most flags, and it was from 'the people' that the most flamboyant suggestions came for monuments. Thus, a correspondent to the *Sunday Express* suggested that 'surely our best war memorial would be a Statue of Liberty on Dover Cliffs showing Mr Churchill facing Europe with folded arms, cigar and all, the cigar to be lit at night. And we should make the Germans build it with marble supplied by the Wops'.

In the hundred days between VE-Day and VJ-Day Churchill was replaced as Prime Minister by Clement Attlee after the election which surprised the world more than it surprised the British, and for a time the famous cigar passed into history. He had not been the first of the war leaders to disappear from the stage. President Roosevelt had died on 12 April on the eve of victory. There had been 'beaming faces' in London when he was returned to power in November 1944 and when

"As far as I'm concerned I don't care if I never see another uniform."

he died Charles Snow reported that he had never seen London 'so devastated' by a single event. Election day (5 July) – D-Day for Democracy – was quieter than the day the results were announced, 26 July. Then there was more elation than there had been in British politics for generations. By comparison VJ-Day (which followed the election and the Bomb) was a victory day which (whatever earlier pessimistic prognostications had been) could be taken almost for granted.

In the VE ITMA broadcast 'VITMA', on 10 May, Mrs Mopp had offered Tommy Handley a V-Day offering which she called 'Peace Pudding'. There were no ironies – and no innuendoes – in his thanks. 'I suppose when you strike your foot in it, it sounds the last "all clear".' Nobody could be sure after the Bomb that if war came again that there would be anyone left to hear a last all-clear.

One entry in a *New Statesman* competition for the best remarks overheard at the Victory celebrations was 'Nice to be again in a pre-war period'.

This book ends not with the peace but with the last 'all clear'. Despite some continuities, 'the age of austerity' after VJ-Day – and it was also, at first, an age of great expectations – was very different from the Second World War itself. 'Don't you know there's a war off?' Handley asked. Even 'cold war', which did not really begin until 1948, was not the same as 'the real thing'.

Some 'things' were rounded off in 1945 so that this book not only does not provide advance notice of the sequel but includes a reprise. On 19 May 1945 *Melody Maker* showed a photograph of the publisher of 'We're Gonna Hang out the Washing on the Siegfried Line' showing a real washing-line hung out across the street from his office bearing the words 'We said we'd hang out the washing on the Siegfried Line.' *Melody Maker* itself was thinking in nobler musical language than a mere reprise: 'In this great symphony of discord,' it wrote in the same week, 'VE-Day is the Coda. Soon the drums of war throughout the world will be stilled, and the calm fluting of a peaceful theme will be stated for the World Orchestra to play. May it be in full harmony.'

With or without the musical accompaniment of a world orchestra, the strains of 'We'll Meet Again' were to be heard everywhere in 1945, though *Picture Post* found it necessary to print an article on 'How to Welcome a Soldier Home', as if the folks at home did not know how to do it. Some of the meetings ended without anybody's guidance (certainly not that of the Ministry of Information) with wedding rings. Other meetings needed more than a wedding ring: 'Well, I suppose that's the end of MY peace. Wish that SWINE o' mine was goin' to Japan. Comin' 'ome with his Hitlerin'. The kids are terrified. Had their own way wi' me and no b — — thrashing – and the fun we 'ad in the Raids.'

'A kiss won't mean "Goodbye" but "Hello to love"', was one of the lines in the song 'When the Lights Go on Again'. But there were as many goodbyes in 1945 as helloes 'all over the world'. A. P. Herbert wrote one of the best of them to introduce a brochure for 'Stage Door Canteen', the opening of a London club for men and women of 'the Allied Navies, Armies and Air Forces' at 201 Piccadilly:

Goodbye GI, Bud, now you know the way,
Come back and see us in a brighter day,
When England's free, and 'Scotch' is cheap but strong,
And you can bring your pretty wives along.

Goodbye GI. Don't leave us quite alone,
Somewhere in England we must write in stone,
'How Britain was Invaded by the Yanks'
And under that a big and hearty 'Thanks'.

'Germany calling'

After D-Day Hitler's anti-British propaganda grew increasingly desperate. In leaflets dropped on Allied troops in Normandy he tried to demoralize British servicemen by showing pictures of American troops at home seducing their wives and sweethearts (*right*). There were also crude appeals to anti-semitism (*above right*), and suggestions that the D in D-Day stood for death (*above*). Another poster (unshown) which might be described as 'Malapropaganda' showed an attractive woman telephoning with the caption, 'Will you ever hear her sweat (sic) voice again?...'

'Somewhere in Southern England'

(The most repeated phrase of summer 1944)

'England is expectant, almost hushed,' wrote J. L. Hodson in his diary on 26 May 1944. 'Every time we turn on the radio we expect to hear that the great invasion of Europe has begun.' Churchill was shown with starting pistol poised by *Daily Mirror* cartoonist Zec as early as 2 May 1944 (*left*), but it was not until 6 June that BBC listeners heard the expected announcement, 'Here is a special bulletin, read by John Snagge. D-Day has come. Early this morning the Allies began the assault on the north-western face of Hitler's European fortress.'

'England floats by under you, those lovely English fields and lakes and woods. The little farm cottages, smothered in the cool, clean morning mist' . . . (Extracts from a letter home by an American bomber pilot in June 1944)

The painting by W. T. Monnington of Spitfires in Southern England, 1944 (*above*) captures the same pastoral mood.

Hush! Here comes a buzz-bomb

'The quickest apple harvest ever'

(Comment by Kent farmer after a V2 fell in his orchard, September 1944)

'*It's ridiculous to say these flying bombs have affected people in ANY way.*'

The Germans had consoled themselves as early as 1943 with thoughts of 'all-annihilating wonder weapons'. Yet the guided V missiles were not despatched until June 1944. They arrived with attendant propaganda: . . . 'Pauseless attacks . . . the South Coast shrouded for days in light and fire' . . . the King off to 'an unknown destination with a view to greater personal safety'. The British preferred VIs (*opposite above*) to V2s – if it came to a choice – but they had advanced far from the opinion expressed by 'a highly placed air authority,' singled out as a 'Blimpism' in the *New Statesman*'s '*This England*' column in February 1940: 'When you realize that 10,000 robot planes . . . can be sent into enemy country by pushing a button, the whole business of aerial warfare becomes a farce.'

'When peace breaks out . . .'

(From a Murphy's advertisement for electric lights, 1941)

1944. "When this foul black-out finally goes I'm going to open every window and turn on every light, and I'm going to go round to every house in the Square and ring the bell and shout ' Put that light on !' "

"Have you boys seen the bad news?"

'When peace breaks out (as it will do you know) and the lights come on again, we shall look back on these days and remember gratefully the things that brought us cheer and gave us heart in even the glummest hours.'

People had been singing 'When the Lights Come on Again' since 1942, but the first lights came on again in 1944 – ironically as the first V2s fell on Southern England. On 17 September 1944 when the blackout gave way to a half-hearted dim-out not many people shared the high spirits of the man in Fougasse's cartoon (*above*). That autumn some railings (wooden only) reappeared around London parks and squares, as George Orwell noted gloomily, and the barbed wire and restrictions began to disappear from Britain's beaches (*opposite above*). Spivs (*above right*) and children (*opposite above*) looked forward apprehensively to the end of the war, and in November the Home Guard – 'the army that never had to fight' – was stood down, to the disgust of many loyal supporters. A month later Harold Nicolson wrote: 'I think that everyone in these dark autumn days is truly unhappy. Partly war weariness, partly sadness at things not going right, and partly actual malnutrition.'

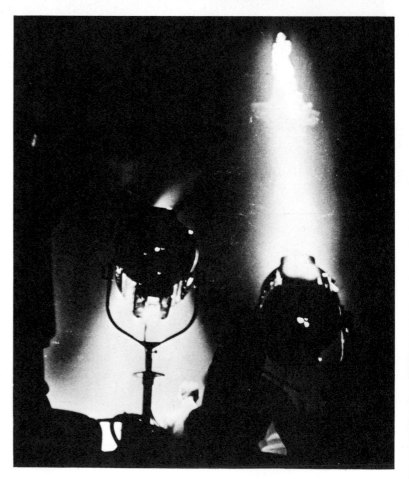

'Who can tell?'

"And one day there won't be any more air-raids or black-outs, and all the shop windows and all the streets will be lit up at night."
"What WILL be the matter, Grandma?"

I'm going to get lit up when the lights go up
    in London,
I'm going to get lit up as I've never been
    before;
You will find me on the tiles, you will find
    me wreathed in smiles,
I'm going to get so lit up I'll be visible for
    miles.
(Lyric of popular song, 1943)

The end of the blackout gave no instant passport to happiness. Indeed many public lighting systems were out of order after such long disuse: perhaps the same applied to people's moods too . . . despite the promise (or threat) of the song.

'Now the lights have gone up along this paradise (around the Albert Hall) the couples will be forced to seek some less public rendezvous for their goodnight kisses', was the comment on the end of the black out reported by a young ATS girl.

"Bill arst me to prepare you for a beard."

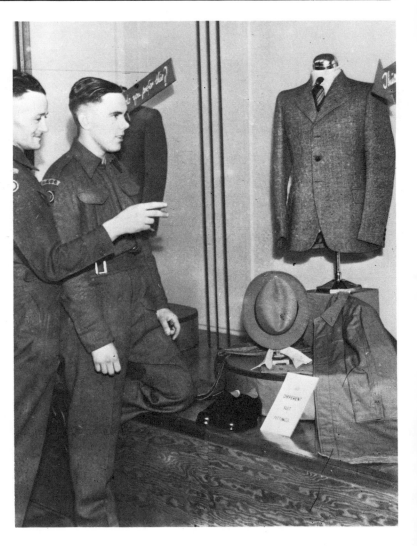

'My husband . . . turned up at 11.30 one night and I had to get out of bed to let him in, trying desperately to get the curlers out of my hair. I'll never forget Bill's face as he stood looking down at his small daughter, whom he was seeing for the first time, and at his son who had grown quite different from the baby he had left behind.' (Woman quoted in Norman Longmate's *How We Lived Then*)

. and Farewell'

"Now be reasonable girls—I can't take you *all* back to the States as stowaways."

'We thank you for all your hospitality, for opening your homes to us, for smiling at us and dancing with us, for marrying some of us, for being patient with our faults, for listening to our talk with tolerance, for struggling with our quaint tongue and then adopting it. For playing host to the vast army of foreigners without letting it get you down. For showing us quiet courage and stamina and the patience that is your greatest virtue and worst handicap. We will remember England.'
(Extract from a letter from a young American soldier. Quoted by Godfrey Winn, 1944)

'The German War is therefore at an end'

(Churchill, broadcasting on VE-Day)

Comments overheard in the crowds on VE night:

'I haven't felt so excited since West Ham won the Cup.'

'. . . . but it would have suited me much better if it had ended last Friday. So far as I'm concerned this war's gone on just three days too long . . .'

'I didn't like paying all that, but we had to have flags. You know how people talk!'

One elderly lady to another: 'Well, I did *think* of buying a small piece of red, white and blue ribbon.'

'When they sound the last All-Clear'

(Song-title)

'Let us join in thanking Almighty God that war has ended throughout the world, and that in every country men may now turn their industry, skill and science to repairing its frightful devastation . . .'
(From the King's broadcast speech to his peoples, VJ-Day, 15 August 1945)

There were a hundred days between the two famous Allied victories, but the street scenes at Piccadilly Circus on VE-Day (*above left*) and at Oxford Circus on VJ-Day (*above right*) look much the same.

'We put out all the flags we had left over from the last war. One of them is the Japanese flag, but what does it matter? It all helps to brighten things up.'
(Woman overheard in Victory celebrations)

'Don't you know there's a war off?'

(Tommy Handley)

The police (*right*) were in expansive mood on VE night . . .These girls (*below*) enjoyed themselves on VE-Day in Piccadilly Circus. So, too, did two other girls, the young princesses, Elizabeth and Margaret who were allowed to join the celebrating crowds near Buckingham Palace. That night the King wrote in his diary, 'Poor darlings, they have never had any fun yet.'

First Woman (in bus): 'Are you getting your flags ready to hang out?'
Second Woman: 'No, we aren't having any flags, there will be no jollification in our family. My sister has lost her son and my other sister's boy is missing.'
First Woman (realizing she had been tactless): 'Yes, it is awful of course. I am not getting any new flags though, only using an old one I had left over from the last war!'

'No, I did not go out on V-Day'

(Bereaved woman quoted by Godfrey Winn in *Scrapbook for Victory*, 1945)

'We are all feeling older' (J. B. Priestley, in a *Postscript* broadcast just after VE-Day)

'It was this enormous sort of anti-climax in a way, it was almost like a bad film, in a way, one of those corny films that you see like Trader Horn . . . and the dead people coming up in the sky afterwards. I saw them all, they all sort of came up in front of me, all their dear faces that . . . died and this was the sort of feeling, of enormous happiness and enormous grief that they had lost their lives so young.' (Woman quoted in BBC *Woman's Hour* programme)

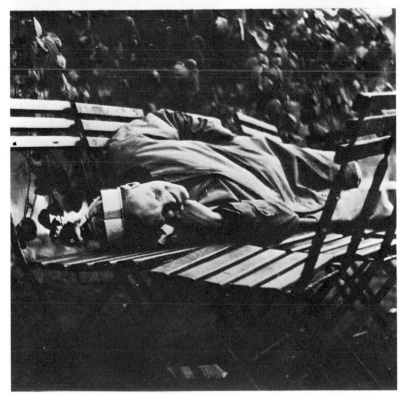

'Now, when you look anxiously into the mirror against his return, you are very conscious of the grey streaks in your hair, the tired lines, a thinness and a sagging that weren't there in the days of unrationed butter and eggs – and no queues. I dare say your first instinct is to try and cover it all up for him. Don't. Don't try to pretend that time has stood still for you, like the princess in the fairy story, waiting to be awakened with a kiss. Each time he came home on short leaves, you rightly tried to disguise from him the efforts entailed in keeping the home together, so that he would go back to his unit feeling every inch a fighting cock. . . . But when at long last it is all over, let your side of the picture be placed alongside his, with not a detail, not a sacrifice spared. It is a story not of sadness, but of riches.' (From *Scrapbook for Victory*, Godfrey Winn, 1945)

'We'll Meet Again'

Returning 'seavacuees' sail home from New York on the *Nieuw Amsterdam* in August 1945. The children look completely Americanized after five years in the United States (*above left*).

'You will find that we are moody. Also, don't be surprised if we just sit and think for an hour, or read a book without turning a page for an hour. We will not eat as much as we used to, but this is due to the natural shrinkage of our stomachs. We shall want to go to dances and parties, but in a great many cases you will find that we shall not be able to stand them for long. In many cases, we shall be rather shy of the opposite sex, not having been in contact with them for so long. That will soon right itself, but at first we may appear awkward through trying to remember our manners . . .

One more warning. Returning, we shall be like convalescents from an illness. As we get better, as all convalescents do, we will pass through a very irritable stage. You must forgive us our faults in this stage and try to help us through as much as you can.' (Extracts from a letter in a Prisoner-of-War news sheet, 1944)

THEY HAVEN'T CHANGED A BIT !

Photographs and illustrations were supplied by, or are reproduced by kind permission of the following (numbers in italics indicate colour illustrations):

Associated Press: 79 (below); Cecil Beaton: 68 (above right); Birmingham Central Library: 83 (above left); Bodleian Library (John Johnson Collection): 46 (above left), 238; BBC: 208 (above right); British Museum: 98 (above); Camera Press/Imperial War Museum: 230 (centre left), 240 (above); The Courier: 225 (below); Daily Express: 19; Daily Mail: title page, 146 (below); Daily Mirror: 239 (below), 244 (above); Fox Photos: 26 (above left & right), 27 (below), 48, 49 (below left), 56 (below), 57 (below left & right), 76, 86, 87, 103 (above left), 115 (below left), 143, 153 (below left), 155 (above), 158 (above right), 159 (below), 163 (below), 176 (above), 187 (above left), 190 (above right), 191 (above); Dennis Gifford: 137, 186; Arthur Guinness, Son & Co: 13 (above right); Trustees of the W. Heath Robinson Estate: 124; Illustrated London News: 28, 58, 84, 107 (below right & above); Imperial War Museum: 13 (left above & below), 14, 15, 24 (right), 25 (above left & right), 30 (right), 33 (above right), 34, 37, 49 (below right), 51 (above left), 52 (above), 53 (below), 54 (above), 56 (above left & right), 59 (above), 60 (below), 67 (above right), 68, 77, 79 (below left), 82, 83 (above left), 85 (above), 95 (above left & right), 101, 102, 104, 116, 117, 118 (above), 119 (below), 122 (below right), 123, 127, 135 (above left), 136 (above), 138 (above), 139 (below), 153 (below right), 154 (below), 155 (below right), 157 (above left), 159 (above), 161 (below left & right), 162 (above right), 164 (above), 165, 166-7, 168, 176 (below right), 177 (above left), 178 (below), 179 (above left), 181 (below), 182, 187 (above right), 188 (above left & right & below right), 189 (above right & below), 190 (below), 195 (above right), 204 (below), 205, 208 (below), 210 (above right), 214 (above left), 225 (above), 226 (above left), 231, 233, 239 (above), 247 (above right & below); Jaeger: 13 (below right); Kent Messenger: 43 (above), 49 (above), 54 (above), 55 (above), 59 (below), 67 (above left), 78 (left above & below), 95 (below), 96 (above left), 106 (below), 120 (above left), 139 (below), 157 (above right), 160 (below), 179 (above left), 180 (above), 181 (above right); Keystone Press: 6, 29 (above & below left), 69 (above right), 70, 75 (below left), 241 (above), 251 (above left); Kobal Collection: 206, 207 (above right); Leeds City Library: 53 (above left), 153 (above), 246 (above); London Express News and Features: 61 (cartoon by David Low by arrangement with the Trustees and the London Evening Standard), 241 (below), 242 (above right), 245 (above), 251 (below); London Museum: 25 (below right), 42 (insert), 44 (above left & below right), 46 (above right & below), 51 (below), 71, 134, 161 (above), 162 (below right); London Transport: 119 (above left), 194 (below left); Mander and Mitchenson Theatre Collection: 51 (above right), 53 (above right), 66 (below right), 68 (above left), 114 (below left), 143 (below left), 160 (above left), 169, 204 (above left), 209, 210 (above left), 211 (below left & right), 212, 218; Mary Evans Picture Library: 44 (below left), 45, 75 (above right), 78 (left), 103 (above right), 107 (below left), 115 (below right), 122 (below left), 135 (above right), 155 (below centre), 162 (above left), 190 (above left), 229 (above right); National Federation of Women's Institutes: 183 (right), 216, 226 (below); National Film Archives: 36 (below right), 72 (above), 105 (below), 196, 202 (below), 207 (above left & below), 208 (above left); Press Association: 50 (below right); Popperphoto: 26 (below), 27 (above), 50 (above), 69 (below), 75 (above left), 114 (centre), 128, 135 (below right), 136 (below), 191 (below), 197 (above right), 228 (above), 229 (below), 230 (above right & below), 244 (below right), 250 (above left); Popperphoto/John Topham: 42 (centre), 52 (below), 55 (below left), 67 (below), 69 (above left), 79 (above right), 97 (above right), 106 (above right), 185 (above right), 211 (above); Popperphoto/United Press International: 30 (left), 71 (below), 74, 80, 105 (above), 154 (above); Punch: 29 (below right), 60 (above), 94, 96 (below), 118 (below), 119 (above right), 120 (above right), 121 (below right), 129, 135 (below left), 140 (below left), 145 (below), 147 (below), 158 (above left), 160 (above right), 163 (above), 164 (below), 178 (above), 195 (below), 203 (above left & below), 226 (above right), 228 (below), 229 (above left), 232, 242 (above left), 243 (below), 244 (below left); Radio Times Hulton Picture Library: 24 (left), 31, 32 (below right & above), 35, 36 (below left & above), 43 (below), 44 (above right), 55 (below left), 72 (below), 73 (below left & right), 77 (below left & right), 79 (above left), 81, 83 (below), 85 (above), 97 (above left & below), 103 (below), 115 (above), 120 (below), 121 (above), 122 (above right), 125, 138 (below), 140 (above & centre), 152, 155 (below left), 156, 177 (left), 180 (below), 185 below), 188 (below left), 189 (above left), 194 (below right), 197, 202 (above left), 204 (above right), 210 (below), 213 (above & below), 214 (above right & below), 215, 216 (above right & below), 217, 227, 240 (below), 242 (below), 243 (above), 245 (below), 246 (below), 247 (above right), 248, 249, 250 (above right), 251 (below), 252; Edward Reeves: 66 (centre); Savoy Hotel: 158 (below); Mary Speaight Collection: 33 (above left & below), 47; D. C. Thomson & Co Ltd., Dundee: 50 (below left), 187 (below), 195 (above left); Carel Toms: 98 (below), 99; Toronto Metropolitan Library: 100, 181 (above left), 100, 224, 251 (above right); Tribune: 219; Victoria and Albert Museum: 256 (design by Einar Forseth); Womens Royal Voluntary Service: 25 (below left), 32 (below left), 73 (above left & right), 106 (above left), 146 (above left & right), 157 (below), 184, 194 (below).

Song lyrics are reproduced by kind permission of the following: Campbell Connelly & Co Ltd: 'There'll Always Be An England' (words and music by Ross Parker and Hughie Charles'), 'We'll Meet Again' and 'When the Lights Go On Again' (words and music by Eddie Seiler, Sol Marcus and Benny Benjemen); Chappell & Co Ltd: 'Don't Fence Me In' (Lyrics by Cole Porter. Copyright © 1944 by Harms Inc. Copyright renewed: All rights reserved), 'It's a Lovely Day Tomorrow' (Lyrics by Irving Berlin), 'Over There' (lyrics by George M. Cohan); B. Feldman & Co Ltd: 'Dig! Dig! Dig! to Victory'; Francis Day & Hunter Ltd: 'Don't Get Around Much Anymore'; Noel Gay Music Company Ltd: 'Hey Little Hen'; Peter Maurice Music Co Ltd: 'We're Gonna Hang Out the Washing On the Siegfried Line', 'Be Like the Kettle and Sing'.

8th June, 1946

To-day, as we celebrate victory, I send this personal message to you and all other boys and girls at school. For you have shared in the hardships and dangers of a total war and you have shared no less in the triumph of the Allied Nations.

I know you will always feel proud to belong to a country which was capable of such supreme effort; proud, too, of parents and elder brothers and sisters who by their courage, endurance and enterprise brought victory. May these qualities be yours as you grow up and join in the common effort to establish among the nations of the world unity and peace.

George R.I.

IMPORTANT
WAR DATES

1939

SEP 1. Germany invaded Poland
SEP 3. Great Britain and France declared war on Germany; the B.E.F. began to leave for France
DEC 13. Battle of the River Plate

1940

APR 9. Germany invaded Denmark and Norway
MAY 10. Germany invaded the Low Countries
JUNE 3. Evacuation from Dunkirk completed
JUNE 8. British troops evacuated from Norway
JUNE 11. Italy declared war on Great Britain
JUNE 22. France capitulated
JUNE 29. Germans occupied the Channel Isles
AUG 8–OCT 31. German air offensive against Great Britain (Battle of Britain)
OCT 28. Italy invaded Greece
NOV 11–12. Successful attack on the Italian Fleet in Taranto Harbour.
DEC 9–11. Italian invasion of Egypt defeated at the battle of Sidi Barrani

1941

MAR 11. Lease-Lend Bill passed in U.S.A.
MAR 28. Battle of Cape Matapan
APR 6. Germany invaded Greece
APR 12–DEC 9. The Siege of Tobruk
MAY 20. Formal surrender of remnants of Italian Army in Abyssinia
MAY 20–31. Battle of Crete
MAY 27. German battleship *Bismarck* sunk
JUNE 22. Germany invaded Russia
AUG 12. Terms of the Atlantic Charter agreed
NOV 18. British offensive launched in the Western Desert
DEC 7. Japanese attacked Pearl Harbour
DEC 8. Great Britain and United States of America declared war on Japan

1942

FEB 15. Fall of Singapore
APR 16. George Cross awarded to Malta
OCT 23–NOV 4. German-Italian army defeated at El Alamein
NOV 8. British and American forces landed in North Africa

1943

JAN 31. The remnants of the 6th German Army surrendered at Stalingrad
MAY Final victory over the U-Boats in the Atlantic
MAY 13. Axis forces in Tunisia surrendered
JULY 10. Allies invaded Sicily
SEP 3. Allies invaded Italy
SEP 8. Italy capitulated
DEC 26. *Scharnhorst* sunk off North Cape

1944

JAN 22. Allied troops landed at Anzio
JUNE 4. Rome captured
JUNE 6. Allies landed in Normandy
JUNE 13. Flying-bomb (V.1) attack on Britain started
JUNE Defeat of Japanese invasion of India
AUG 25. Paris liberated
SEP 3. Brussels liberated
SEP 8. The first rocket-bomb (V.2) fell on England.
SEP 17–26. The Battle of Arnhem
OCT 20. The Americans re-landed in the Philippines

1945

JAN 17. Warsaw liberated
MAR 20. British recaptured Mandalay
MAR 23. British crossed the Rhine
APR 25. Opening of Conference of United Nations at San Francisco
MAY 2. German forces in Italy surrendered
MAY 3. Rangoon recaptured
MAY 5. All the German forces in Holland, N.W. Germany and Denmark surrendered unconditionally
MAY 9. Unconditional surrender of Germany to the Allies ratified in Berlin
JUNE 10. Australian troops landed in Borneo
AUG 6. First atomic bomb dropped on Hiroshima
AUG 8. Russia declared war on Japan
AUG 9. Second atomic bomb dropped on Nagasaki
AUG 14. The Emperor of Japan broadcast the unconditional surrender of his country
SEP 5. British forces re-entered Singapore

MY FAMILY'S WAR RECORD

Ah! but victory is no conclusion; even final victory will only open a new and happier field of valiant endeavour.

(Churchill, 14 May 1943)

Susan Briggs would like to thank the following individuals and organizations for their generous help: The University of Sussex Library, the Brighton Public Reference Library, Leeds City Reference Library, Metropolitan Toronto Central Library, Hastings Public Reference Library. Miss Kurkiewicz of the Local Studies Department of the Birmingham Public Library, the Curator and staff of the Southampton Civic Records Office, Marjorie Willis of the Radio Times Hulton Picture Library, Mr Tom Harrisson and the staff of the Mass Observation Archive, University of Sussex. Mr Brian Spencer, Mr Colin Sorensen, Mrs Mary Speaight and Mr Christopher Newberry of the London Museum, Mr Simmons, Mrs Murray, Mr Mike Moody, Mr Barry Kitts and the staff of the Film Department of the Imperial War Museum, Mrs Madeleine Ginsberg and the staff of the Textiles Department of the Victoria and Albert Museum, Mr Jeremy Boulton of the British Film Institute, the staff of the John Johnson Collection at the Bodleian Library, Oxford and of the NAAFI Museum. Dame Frances Clode and Mrs Doreen Harris and her colleagues in the archives of the WRVS Headquarters, Miss V. Royds of the NFWI Headquarters and Miss M. Walton and the staff of the East Sussex Branch of the NFWI, Lord Moyne and the staff of the Dublin and Park Royal Breweries of Arthur Guinness, Son & Co, the Savoy Hotel, Mr Keith Wilson of the University of Sussex Photo/Graphic Unit. The Editor of *Punch*, Mr Peter Senn, Mr Mike Molloy and Mr Clifford Davis of the *Daily Mirror*, Mr Brian Thomson of D. C. Thomson & Co. Ltd., Dundee, Mr Roy Birchall and Mr Tony Claxton of *Melody Maker*, Mr Reg Smith of the *Illustrated London News*, Mr Stan Gallavin and his colleagues at the *Kent Messenger*. Miss Hilary Arnold, Sir Michael Balcon, Sir Cecil Beaton and his secretary Miss Eileen Hose, Mrs Ernestine Carter, Lord Clark of Saltwood, Simon Dally, Dennis Gifford, Geoff Goode, Raymond Mander and Joe Mitchenson, Mr Digby Morton, Mr Charles Ritchie, Mr Kenneth Rose, Mrs Alison Settle, Miss Eileen Tweedy, Mr David Toff.